Exploring the Extraordinary

500 Fun Facts to Amaze and Intrigue

Michael Brancati

Contents

Chapter One
Forgotten Civilizations

The Vinca Culture: Europe's Prehistoric Metropolis

The Vinča culture, which thrived from around 5700 to 4500 BC in what is now the Balkans, is notable for its early use of metallurgy and urban planning. Remarkably, it produced some of Europe's first copper artifacts, predating other known developments in metallurgy. Additionally, the archaeological sites associated with this culture, particularly the one at Vinča-Belo Brdo near Belgrade, reveal evidence of well-organized settlements with houses made of wattle and daub, suggesting a sophisticated understanding of urban living.

The Mysterious Indus Valley Civilization

The Indus Valley Civilization (3300 to 1300 BCE) demonstrated remarkable hydraulic engineering prowess. This ancient society developed an advanced urban water management system, complete with covered drains and sewage systems, in cities such as Mohenjo-Daro and Harappa. Their drainage systems were so sophisticated that they surpassed those of many contemporary urban centers, highlighting their early understanding of sanitation and public health.

The Kingdom of Aksum: An Ancient African Power

The Kingdom of Aksum, an ancient African power that flourished between the 1st and 8th centuries AD in what is now Ethiopia and Eritrea, was among the first major empires in the world to officially adopt Christianity. By the 4th century AD, under King Ezana, Aksum not only embraced Christianity but also minted coins bearing the cross, symbolizing its official state religion. This early conversion played a crucial role in shaping the religious landscape of the region, influencing the development of Ethiopian Orthodox Christian traditions that persist to this day.

The Sogdian Civilization: Merchants of the Silk Road

The Sogdian civilization, active from the 6th century BC to the 11th century AD, was renowned for its traders and merchants who dominated the Silk Road. These Sogdian merchants were instrumental in facilitating the exchange of goods, ideas, and cultures between the East and West. Their influence was so profound that Sogdian became the lingua franca of the Silk Road, enabling communication and commerce across diverse civilizations spanning from China to the Byzantine Empire.

The Khmer Empire: Southeast Asia's Powerhouse

The Khmer Empire, which ruled much of Southeast Asia from the 9th to the 15th centuries, engineered the largest pre-industrial urban center in the world at its peak. The heart of this empire was Angkor, a mega-city that sprawled over at least 1,000 square kilometers, supported by an intricate system of reservoirs and canals. This hydraulic infrastructure not only sustained large-scale agriculture but also helped the Khmer manage monsoon waters, which was crucial for their rice cultivation.

The Elamite Kingdom: Ancient Iran's Enigmatic Culture

The Elamite Kingdom, an ancient civilization in what is now southwestern Iran, was distinguished by its development of one of the world's earliest scripts, known as Elamite cuneiform. Emerging around 2200 BC, this writing system was initially adapted from the Sumerian cuneiform but evolved to meet the specific linguistic needs of the Elamites. This script was crucial for administrative and ceremonial purposes, underscoring the sophisticated bureaucratic system that characterized Elamite culture.

The Minoan Civilization: Crete's Bronze Age Marvel

The Minoan civilization, centered on the island of Crete during the Bronze Age, is credited with creating the first advanced maritime network in the Mediterranean. Flourishing from approximately 2700 to 1450 BC, the Minoans built an extensive trade system that connected them with Egypt, the Cycladic Islands, the Greek mainland, and as far west as Sicily. This network not only facilitated the exchange of goods like saffron, pottery, and precious metals but also enabled the spread of cultural and technological innovations across the region.

The Hittite Empire: Anatolia's Forgotten Superpower

The Hittite Empire, which reached its peak in the 14th century BC in what is now modern Turkey, was one of the earliest cultures to use iron. This innovation gave them a significant military advantage, allowing them to forge stronger weapons than their Bronze Age contemporaries. The Hittites' mastery of ironworking not only played a pivotal role in their military successes but also marked a key development in the technological evolution from the Bronze to the Iron Age.

The Urartian Kingdom: Masters of the Armenian Highlands

The Urartian Kingdom, thriving between the 9th and 6th centuries BC in the Armenian Highlands, was renowned for its advanced water management techniques. They constructed sophisticated irrigation networks and massive reservoirs, one of the most famous being the Menua Canal, named after King Menua who expanded it. This canal was not only a feat of engineering but also essential for agriculture, significantly boosting the region's crop yields and supporting the kingdom's prosperity.

The Nabatean Kingdom: Architects of Petra

The Nabatean Kingdom, known for the architectural marvel of Petra, also excelled in water conservation technologies in their arid desert environment. They developed a complex system of dams, cisterns, and water channels to capture and store every possible drop of rainwater. This ingenuity in water management enabled the Nabateans to thrive in the desert and transform Petra into a bustling trade hub and a testament to their architectural and engineering prowess.

The Mississippian Culture: North America's Mound Builders

The Mississippian culture, which flourished from around 800 to 1600 AD across the central United States, is renowned for its large earthen mounds. The largest of these, Monk's Mound at Cahokia, near present-day St. Louis, Missouri, covers over 14 acres and rises to a height of about 100 feet. It is the largest prehistoric earthen construction in the Americas and served as the ceremonial and political center of the Cahokia complex, underscoring the sophistication and social organization of the Mississippian peoples.

The Tiwanaku Empire: Andean Pre-Inca Civilization

The Tiwanaku Empire, an influential pre-Inca civilization centered around Lake Titicaca in Bolivia, developed from 300 to 1000 AD and displayed exceptional skill in agricultural innovation. They invented the raised field system, known as "suka kollus," which improved drainage and soil fertility. This technique allowed them to cultivate crops at altitudes previously deemed unsuitable for agriculture, significantly expanding their agricultural output and sustaining a large population in the harsh Andean highlands.

The Kingdom of Funan: Southeast Asia's Ancient Maritime Power

The Kingdom of Funan, one of Southeast Asia's earliest historical states from the 1st to 6th centuries AD, was a major maritime power situated along the Mekong Delta. Funan is notable for its early adoption of Sanskrit as an administrative language, evidence of intense cultural and trade exchanges with India. This interaction facilitated the spread of Hinduism and Buddhism in the region, alongside the introduction of advanced Indian agricultural techniques, which significantly influenced the local cultures and economies.

The Silla Kingdom: One of Korea's Three Kingdoms

The Silla Kingdom, one of Korea's Three Kingdoms, ruled from 57 BC to 935 AD and is celebrated for unifying the Korean Peninsula in 668 AD. This unification under Silla's rule was a significant historical milestone, leading to a period of peace and cultural flourishing known as the Unified Silla era. During this time, Silla artisans crafted exquisite gold crowns and jewelry, demonstrating sophisticated metalworking skills that reflect the kingdom's wealth and artistic heritage.

The Kushan Empire: Central Asia's Cultural Melting Pot

The Kushan Empire, which flourished from the 1st to the 3rd centuries AD in what is now northern India, Afghanistan, and parts of Central Asia, played a pivotal role in the Silk Road's history. This empire was a cultural melting pot, significantly facilitating the spread of ideas, technologies, and religious beliefs between the East and West. The Kushans were instrumental in the spread of Buddhism into China and the development of the Gandhara School of Art, which blended Greek, Persian, and Indian artistic influences, creating a unique and influential artistic style.

The Bactrian Civilization: Crossroads of the Ancient World

The Bactrian civilization, centered in what is now modern-day Afghanistan, thrived as a crucial hub on the Silk Road from the 3rd to the 2nd century BC. This region, known for its wealth and cultural diversity, was often called the "Crossroads of the Ancient World." Bactria's strategic location facilitated not only the trade of goods like silk and spices but also an extraordinary exchange of cultural and intellectual ideas, contributing significantly to the artistic and scholarly advancements during the Hellenistic period.

The Anasazi and Their Cliff Dwellings

The Anasazi, also known as the Ancestral Puebloans, are renowned for their cliff dwellings, which are among the most striking and enduring features of their culture. Built between 900 and 1300 AD in what is now the Southwestern United States, these structures were strategically nestled in alcoves high in the sandstone cliffs. This placement provided natural insulation against the harsh desert climate and enhanced defenses against potential invaders. The most famous of these complexes, Mesa Verde, contains over 600 cliff dwellings, illustrating the Anasazi's ingenuity in architecture and their ability to adapt to their environment.

The Olmec Civilization: Mesoamerica's First Great Culture

The Olmec civilization, known as Mesoamerica's first great culture and flourishing from around 1200 to 400 BC, is famed for its colossal head sculptures. Carved from single blocks of basalt, these heads can reach up to 3 meters in height and weigh several tons. They are believed to represent the Olmec rulers and demonstrate not only the skill and technological prowess of Olmec artisans but also the significant effort and resources dedicated to their leaders' cults.

The Nok Culture: West Africa's Early Iron Age Society

The Nok culture, an early Iron Age society that emerged in what is now Nigeria around 1500 BC and lasted until about 500 AD, is renowned for its terracotta sculptures. These artifacts are among the earliest examples of figurative art in sub-Saharan Africa and are characterized by their highly stylized features and intricate detailing. The terracottas provide valuable insights into the cultural practices, religious beliefs, and social structures of the Nok people, highlighting their advanced artistic and technological capabilities long before many other civilizations adopted similar techniques.

The Caral-Supe Civilization: America's First Urban Centers

The Caral-Supe civilization, which thrived along the coast of Peru around 3000 BC, is recognized as one of the oldest urban centers in the Americas. A standout feature of this ancient society is its monumental architecture, including large pyramidal structures and sunken circular plazas. These architectural achievements are notable not only for their scale and sophistication but also because they were constructed nearly a millennium before the pyramids of Egypt, underscoring Caral-Supe's importance in the development of early urban civilizations globally.

The Gandhara Kingdom: A Fusion of Greek and Buddhist Art

The Gandhara Kingdom, located in what is now modern-day Pakistan and Afghanistan, became a unique melting pot of cultures following Alexander the Great's invasion in the 4th century BC. This region is particularly celebrated for its distinctive art form, Gandharan art, which emerged from the fusion of Greek artistic techniques with Buddhist themes. The most iconic Gandharan artworks are the Buddhist statues that display clear Hellenistic influences, such as the draping of robes and the realistic treatment of human bodies, marking a significant cultural and artistic synthesis between East and West.

The Parthian Empire: Rome's Eastern Rival

The Parthian Empire, which lasted from 247 BC to AD 224, was known for its formidable cavalry, especially the "cataphracts" — heavily armored horsemen who could withstand prolonged combat against Roman forces. This military innovation not only made the Parthians a significant threat to Rome but also influenced Roman military tactics. The Parthians were also adept at using a technique known as the "Parthian shot," where archers on horseback would feign retreat and then turn their bodies to shoot arrows while still in full gallop, a maneuver that became legendary in the annals of warfare.

The Scythians: Nomads of the Eurasian Steppe

The Scythians, nomadic warriors who roamed the Eurasian steppes from around the 9th century BC to the 1st century AD, were renowned for their skills in mounted archery. Their mastery of horseback combat was so advanced that they could accurately shoot arrows at full gallop, a technique that was crucial for their dominance over vast territories from the Black Sea to China. This prowess not only made them feared opponents in battle but also significantly influenced the military strategies of neighboring civilizations.

The Dacian Kingdom: Rome's Fierce Adversaries

The Dacian Kingdom, located in what is now Romania, was recognized for its fierce resistance against the Roman Empire until it was finally conquered by Emperor Trajan in 106 AD. A notable aspect of Dacian culture was their sophisticated metalworking, particularly in gold. They were skilled at creating intricate jewelry and weapons, which suggests a high level of technological and artistic achievement. The wealth generated from their gold mines was a significant factor in the prosperity of their civilization and a key motive behind Rome's campaigns to conquer them.

The Lydian Kingdom: Inventors of Coinage

The Lydian Kingdom, which thrived in western Turkey around 700 BC, is credited with inventing the world's first coinage. This innovation marked a significant development in economic history, facilitating trade and commerce by providing a standardized medium of exchange. The Lydians' coins, made from electrum, a natural alloy of gold and silver, were stamped with official marks to certify their authenticity, thereby introducing the concept of guaranteed value in monetary transactions.

The Nabataeans: Architects of the Desert

The Nabataeans, an ancient Arab people who inhabited northern Arabia and the Southern Levant, were masterful architects, famously known for sculpting the city of Petra directly into the rose-colored sandstone cliffs. Beyond their architectural prowess, they excelled in water conservation within their arid environment. They developed an extensive system of dams, cisterns, and water conduits, which cleverly collected and stored rainwater, thus sustaining their urban settlements in the harsh desert landscape and enabling their culture to flourish from the 4th century BC until about the 1st century AD.

The Axumite Empire: Africa's Christian Kingdom

The Axumite Empire, an ancient African kingdom located in what is now Ethiopia and Eritrea, was one of the first major empires in the world to convert to Christianity. This transition occurred in the early 4th century AD under King Ezana, who adopted Christianity shortly after the Roman Emperor Constantine the Great. The adoption significantly influenced Axum's culture and administration, leading to the creation of unique Christian inscriptions and monumental architecture, including the famous stelae or obelisks, which were intricately carved and stood as high as 24 meters.

The Cucuteni-Trypillia Culture: Europe's Prehistoric Megalopolis

The Cucuteni-Trypillia culture, which flourished between 5500 BC and 2750 BC in what is now Romania, Moldova, and Ukraine, is notable for having some of the largest Neolithic settlements ever discovered in Europe. At their peak, these settlements could house between 10,000 to 15,000 inhabitants, a size that rivals that of contemporary urban centers in the Near East. Remarkably, these large communities were built with dense clusters of multi-storied buildings and are known for their distinctive pottery with intricate, colorful designs, showcasing a sophisticated level of social organization and artistic development long before the rise of classical civilizations in Europe.

The Sea Peoples: Enigmatic Raiders of the Bronze Age

The Sea Peoples, a confederation of naval raiders who troubled the Eastern Mediterranean at the end of the Bronze Age around the 12th century BC, played a pivotal role in the downfall of several ancient civilizations, including the Hittites and Egyptians. These mysterious groups are often credited with causing widespread disruption that led to the collapse of the Bronze Age. Despite their significant impact on history, the precise origins and composition of the Sea Peoples remain largely unknown, as they appear prominently in Egyptian records primarily as formidable adversaries in battle.

The Thracian Civilization: Warriors and Artists of the Balkans

The Thracian civilization, which existed from about 2000 BC until being absorbed by the Roman Empire in the 1st century AD, was renowned not only for its fierce warriors but also for its rich artistic traditions. Thrace, located in the Balkans, was particularly noted for its exquisite metalwork, especially in silver and gold. The Thracians created highly decorative and ceremonial objects, including elaborate funerary masks and intricately designed jewelry, which were esteemed for their craftsmanship across the ancient world and significantly influenced the art of their neighbors, including the Greeks.

The Muisca Confederation: The Eldorado Legend

The Muisca Confederation, which flourished in the highlands of present-day Colombia before the Spanish conquest, is often associated with the legend of El Dorado. This legend stems from the Muisca ritual of the zipa (leader), who would cover himself in gold dust during ceremonies and then dive into Lake Guatavita to wash it off. The spectacle of gold offerings thrown into the lake to appease the gods captured the imagination of the Spanish conquistadors, fueling relentless quests for a city of gold in the Americas and deeply embedding the myth of El Dorado in popular lore.

The Sarmatians: Iranic Nomads of the Steppes

The Sarmatians, an Iranic group of nomadic tribes from the Eurasian steppes, flourished from around the 5th century BC to the 4th century AD. They were renowned for their fierce female warriors, who are believed to have inspired the Greek myths of the Amazons. Archaeological evidence, including burials with women interred with weapons and armor, suggests that Sarmatian women participated actively in horseback riding and combat. This egalitarian aspect of their society was noted by ancient historians and remains a significant aspect of Sarmatian cultural identity.

The Zapotec Civilization: Pioneers of Oaxaca

The Zapotec civilization, emerging around 700 BC in the Valley of Oaxaca, Mexico, was an early Mesoamerican culture known for creating the first writing system in the Americas. The Zapotecs developed a series of glyphs, similar in function to Egyptian hieroglyphs, which were used to inscribe monuments and codices. This script was instrumental in documenting events, rituals, and genealogies, playing a crucial role in the administration of their city-states and in the continuity of their cultural practices.

The Kingdom of Kush: Nubia's Ancient Empire

The Kingdom of Kush, situated along the Nile River just south of Ancient Egypt, was a powerful empire from around 1070 BC to AD 350. One of its most striking features was the construction of pyramids as tombs for their kings and queens, similar to, but distinct from, those of their Egyptian neighbors. The Kushites built more pyramids than the Egyptians, albeit smaller in size, with steep angles and smaller bases, predominantly located in the necropolises of Meroë, which remains a testament to their architectural ingenuity and cultural richness.

The Tartessos Civilization: Iberia's Ancient Traders

The Tartessos civilization, which thrived in southern Iberia from around 1100 to 500 BC, is recognized for its wealth and advanced trade networks. Tartessos was one of the earliest cultures in Western Europe to engage in trade with the Phoenicians, exchanging local resources like silver, gold, and tin for eastern luxuries and innovations. This interaction facilitated not only economic prosperity but also the flow of cultural and technological influences, notably including the introduction of the Phoenician alphabet, which significantly impacted the development of writing in Iberia.

The Tiahuanaco Culture: Pre-Inca Andean Innovators

The Tiahuanaco culture, which thrived around Lake Titicaca in the Andes from 300 AD to 1000 AD, was highly advanced in its agricultural practices, notably in the development of the raised field system, known as "suka kollus." These artificially constructed platforms of soil elevated above the floodplain allowed for enhanced temperature regulation and moisture retention, significantly boosting crop yields in the harsh Andean climate. This innovative farming technique not only sustained large populations but also exemplifies the Tiahuanaco's sophisticated understanding of their environment.

The Cahokia Mounds: A Pre-Columbian Native American City

Cahokia Mounds, located in modern-day Illinois, was once the largest pre-Columbian settlement north of Mexico, flourishing between 600 and 1400 AD. This site was home to one of the most significant earthwork structures, Monk's Mound, which covers 14 acres and rises to a height of about 100 feet. Cahokia's sophisticated city layout included over 120 mounds and a carefully planned urban center with a central plaza, indicating a high level of social organization and political structure unique to Native American cultures of the period.

The Maurya Empire: India's First Imperial Power

The Maurya Empire, established in 322 BC by Chandragupta Maurya, was India's first imperial power and marked a significant period of political and economic unity in the region. Under the reign of Ashoka the Great, the empire expanded to cover most of the

Indian subcontinent. Ashoka is particularly renowned for his widespread promotion of Buddhism after his conversion following the bloody Kalinga war. His efforts to spread Buddhist principles were carved into pillars and rocks across his empire, known as the Edicts of Ashoka, which serve as some of the oldest deciphered original writings of Indian history.

The Guanches: Mysterious Inhabitants of the Canary Islands

The Guanches were the indigenous people of the Canary Islands before the Spanish conquest in the 15th century. Intriguingly, they practiced a form of mummification similar to that of the ancient Egyptians. The Guanches mummified their dead using techniques that preserved the bodies with remarkable effectiveness, considering the islands' humid climate. These mummies were then placed in burial caves located in cliffs or volcanic craters, highlighting a complex ritual and societal respect for the deceased that provides insights into their unique cultural practices.

The Xiongnu Confederation: Nomadic Rivals of Ancient China

The Xiongnu Confederation, a powerful nomadic group from the steppes of Central Asia, emerged as a significant threat to ancient China around the 3rd century BC. Their military prowess and organized society prompted the Chinese to construct and expand the Great Wall, aiming to protect their borders from Xiongnu raids. The Xiongnu were among the first to use complex military strategies involving large numbers of mounted archers, showcasing their advanced understanding of mobility and warfare in the vast terrains of the steppes.

The Yayoi Culture: Ancestors of Japan

The Yayoi culture, which emerged around 300 BC in Japan, marked a significant transition from the Jomon period with the introduction of wet-rice agriculture. This advancement brought about profound changes in Japanese society, facilitating population growth and the formation of larger, more complex social structures. The Yayoi are also credited with the introduction of metalworking, particularly in bronze and iron, which led to the development of weapons and tools far superior to those of the preceding eras.

These technological innovations not only altered daily life but also laid the foundations for the future social and political landscape of Japan.

The Chachapoyas Culture: The Cloud Warriors of Peru

The Chachapoyas, known as the "Cloud Warriors," inhabited the cloud forests of northern Peru before the Inca conquest in the 15th century. They are famous for their unique burial practices, particularly the construction of cliffside tombs and sarcophagi. These tombs, high up in the mountain cliffs, often feature mummies placed in a seated position, facing out over the landscape. This method of burial not only protected the remains from looters but also reflected the Chachapoyas' deep respect for their ancestors, ensuring they maintained a symbolic watch over their lands.

The Urnfield Culture: Bronze Age Europe's Mystery

The Urnfield culture, which dominated Central Europe from around 1300 to 750 BC, is named after its unique burial practice of cremating the dead and placing their ashes in urns. These urns were then buried in fields, giving rise to the culture's name. This practice marked a significant shift from the previous traditions of elaborate burials with grave goods. The widespread adoption of cremation reflects broader changes in societal structures and religious beliefs during the European Bronze Age, illustrating a move towards more uniform cultural practices across large areas.

The Chimú Civilization: Pre-Columbian Artisans of Peru

The Chimú civilization, which thrived along the northern coast of Peru before being conquered by the Incas in the late 15th century, was renowned for its highly skilled artisans and advanced metallurgical techniques. They excelled particularly in the craftsmanship of intricate silver and gold work, which included stunning jewelry and religious items. The Chimú also developed a sophisticated irrigation system for their arid environment, enabling them to cultivate extensive agricultural fields and support a large urban population centered in their capital, Chan Chan, one of the largest adobe cities in the ancient world.

The Yamnaya Culture: Steppe Ancestors of Indo-Europeans

The Yamnaya culture, which emerged around 3300–2600 BC in the Pontic-Caspian steppe, is recognized as a significant progenitor of the Indo-European languages, one of the world's largest language families. Genetic studies suggest that the Yamnaya people's migrations across Europe and Asia had a profound demographic impact, spreading not only their language but also their distinctive burial practices and pastoral lifestyle. Their use of horse-drawn chariots facilitated rapid and wide-reaching movements across vast territories, which fundamentally altered the genetic and cultural landscape of prehistoric Europe and Asia.

The Syro-Hittite States: Successors of the Hittite Empire

The Syro-Hittite states, which emerged in the aftermath of the Hittite Empire's collapse around 1200 BC, were a group of polities that thrived in what is now modern-day Turkey and Syria. These states are notable for their vibrant artistic expressions, particularly in the form of monumental stone sculptures and orthostats. Their unique art and architecture feature a blend of Mesopotamian, Anatolian, and Hittite influences, reflecting the cultural melting pot of the region. The Syro-Hittite states played a crucial role in the transmission of Hittite traditions and practices well into the Iron Age, preserving the legacy of Hittite artistic and architectural styles in the ancient Near East.

The Moche Civilization: Peru's Pre-Inca Masters

The Moche civilization, which flourished along the northern coast of Peru between 100 and 800 AD, is particularly noted for its extraordinary pottery. Moche artisans created ceramic vessels that were not only utilitarian but also works of art, vividly depicting a wide range of subjects from daily life, religious rituals, and mythological scenes to complex portrayals of animals and human figures. These ceramics are highly valued for their detailed realism and the insights they provide into Moche culture, including their practices of human sacrifice and complex social ceremonies.

The Gojoseon Kingdom: Korea's Legendary First State

The Gojoseon Kingdom, considered the first state-like entity in Korean history, is traditionally said to have been founded in 2333 BC by the legendary figure Dangun. A fascinating aspect of Gojoseon is its reputed establishment of a centralized government and the introduction of bronze technology, which marked a significant advancement in the region's social and technological development. The legend of Dangun not only underscores Gojoseon's historical importance but also serves as a cultural foundation story for Korea, symbolizing the beginning of Korean civilization and national identity.

The Toltec Civilization: Central Mexico's Cultural Forerunners

The Toltec civilization, which dominated Central Mexico from about 900 to 1150 AD, is often regarded as a precursor to later Mesoamerican cultures, notably the Aztecs, who revered the Toltecs as their intellectual and cultural predecessors. One of the most notable achievements of the Toltecs was their architectural prowess, exemplified by the grand pyramids and palatial complexes at their capital, Tula. These structures prominently featured colossal stone warrior statues, known as "Atlantean figures," that stood atop the pyramids, symbolizing Toltec military might and artistic sophistication.

The Sican Culture: Peru's Goldsmiths of the North

The Sican Culture, which thrived in what is now northern Peru between approximately 750 and 1375 AD, excelled in metallurgy, particularly in the crafting of gold artifacts. Their goldsmiths developed sophisticated techniques for smelting, alloying, and hammering gold, which were used to create intricate jewelry, ceremonial masks, and religious icons. Notably, Sican artisans are known for their distinctive funerary masks, which often feature a radiant sunburst pattern around the face, reflecting their worship of the sun god and their beliefs in the afterlife. These artifacts underscore the Sican's advanced understanding of metal properties and their cultural emphasis on elaborate burial rites.

Chapter Two

Astronomical Oddities

55 Cancri e: The Diamond Planet

55 Cancri e, an exoplanet located about 40 light-years away in the constellation Cancer, stands out due to its probable composition. It is often referred to as a "super-Earth" because of its size—about twice the size of Earth with eight times its mass. What makes 55 Cancri e particularly intriguing is that it is speculated to have a surface composed largely of graphite and diamond, making up as much as a third of its mass. This exotic composition suggests a landscape vastly different from any found in our solar system, reflecting the unique and diverse planetary formations that exist in our galaxy.

Rogue Planets

Rogue planets, also known as free-floating planets, are celestial bodies that do not orbit a star but instead wander through space on their own. These intriguing objects can be as massive as Jupiter or as small as Earth. What makes rogue planets particularly fascinating is that despite their isolation from a stellar light source, some scientists hypothesize they could potentially harbor life. The key lies in the possibility that these planets may maintain heat through radioactive decay or possess insulating atmospheres that trap residual heat from their formation, creating conditions that could support subsurface life.

The Boomerang Nebula

The Boomerang Nebula, located approximately 5,000 light-years away from Earth in the constellation Centaurus, holds the distinction of being the coldest naturally occurring place currently known in the Universe. It boasts temperatures of just 1 degree Kelvin (-272.15 degrees Celsius or -457.87 degrees Fahrenheit), colder than the background temperature of space itself. This remarkable cold is due to the nebula's rapid expansion, which causes the gas it ejects to cool dramatically. Its distinct shape, resembling a boomerang or bow tie, and its extreme temperature make it a subject of significant interest in astronomical studies.

Hyper-Velocity Stars

Hyper-velocity stars are a rare class of stars that travel at speeds so high, they exceed the escape velocity of the Milky Way galaxy. These stars can move faster than 1 million miles per hour, propelled by interactions with the supermassive black hole at the center of our galaxy or through other dynamic celestial events. What makes hyper-velocity stars particularly intriguing is their ability to provide insights into the gravitational forces at play within the galaxy and the dynamics of star clusters and black holes. Their high velocities suggest they are not bound by the galaxy's gravity and are instead hurtling through intergalactic space.

Cosmic Cannibalism

Cosmic cannibalism describes the process where larger galaxies absorb smaller ones through gravitational forces, a common occurrence in the universe's evolution. This galactic interaction leads to the growth of massive galaxies while smaller ones either merge completely or shred into streams of stars. One of the most famous examples of cosmic cannibalism involves the Milky Way, which is currently absorbing several smaller galaxies, such as the Sagittarius Dwarf Spheroidal galaxy. This process provides crucial insights into how galaxies evolve and grow over billions of years.

The Himiko Blob

The Himiko Blob, named after a legendary ancient Japanese queen, is a colossal gas cloud found in the early universe, approximately 12.9 billion light-years away. Discovered through observations with the Subaru Telescope, this mysterious blob is one of the largest objects of its kind ever identified in the distant universe, spanning about 55,000 light-years. What makes the Himiko Blob especially fascinating is its enigmatic nature; despite its massive size, the source of its intense luminosity and the processes powering it remain poorly understood, challenging existing theories about the formation and evolution of galaxies in the early stages of the universe.

Zombie Stars

Zombie stars are an extraordinary astronomical phenomenon where a white dwarf star manages to survive a supernova explosion. Typically, a supernova signifies the catastrophic end of a star, but in rare cases, the white dwarf can siphon enough material from a companion star to approach the critical mass for igniting a supernova, yet not completely disintegrate in the process. This leads to what astronomers refer to as a "zombie star," a star that has come back from the dead. Observations of these stars provide valuable insights into the behavior of supernovae and the life cycle of stars.

The Great Attractor

The Great Attractor is a gravitational anomaly located roughly 250 million light-years away in the intergalactic space within the Laniakea Supercluster. Despite being obscured by the Milky Way's galactic plane, it exerts a massive gravitational pull on the galaxies around it, including our own. This mysterious region is thought to contain a mass equivalent to tens of thousands of Milky Ways, influencing the motions of galaxies over a region hundreds of millions of light-years across. The precise nature and composition of the Great Attractor remain largely unknown, making it one of the most intriguing mysteries in cosmology.

Hoag's Object

Hoag's Object is a peculiar galaxy located approximately 600 million light-years away, noted for its strikingly unusual ring-like appearance. Discovered in 1950 by astronomer Arthur Hoag, the galaxy consists of a nearly perfect circular outer ring surrounding a bright core, separated by a dark void. The ring is packed with blue, young stars, contrasting sharply with the older, yellow stars of the core. This rare formation challenges traditional understandings of galactic structures and is one of only a few known galaxies of its kind, making Hoag's Object a fascinating subject in the study of cosmic formations.

WASP-76b: The Planet with Iron Rain

WASP-76b, an exoplanet located about 640 light-years away in the constellation Pisces, is known for its extreme atmospheric conditions, most notably its iron rain. This gas giant is tidally locked, with one side perpetually facing its host star, receiving temperatures exceeding 2,400 degrees Celsius (4,352 degrees Fahrenheit). This intense heat vaporizes metals like iron on the planet's dayside. As strong winds carry these iron vapors to the cooler night side, they condense into droplets, creating a bizarre weather phenomenon of iron rain. This unique characteristic highlights the diverse and extreme environments that exist on planets beyond our solar system.

Dark Matter Bridges

Dark matter bridges are fascinating structures that consist of filaments of dark matter, which interconnect galaxies across vast cosmic distances. These invisible bridges, detected through gravitational effects on visible matter and radiation, form part of the cosmic web that structures the universe. Research using advanced techniques like weak gravitational lensing has revealed that these dark matter filaments are denser and more structured than previously thought, playing a crucial role in the evolution of galaxy clusters and the overall architecture of the cosmos.

PN M2-9: The Double Jet Nebula

The Double Jet Nebula, formally known as PN M2-9, is a striking example of a bipolar planetary nebula. Located about 4,000 light-years away, it is distinguished by its two symmetrical jets of gas and dust that extend in opposite directions from its central star. This remarkable symmetry creates a visual effect that resembles the wings of a butterfly or the hourglass shape often depicted in artistic representations of nebulas. The formation of these jets is influenced by the complex interactions of stellar winds from the dying central star, which collide and shape the surrounding material into this unique and visually captivating structure.

The Largest Water Reservoir

The largest known water reservoir in the universe is located in a quasar over 12 billion light-years away, surrounding a supermassive black hole at the center of a distant galaxy. This vast cosmic reservoir contains a mass of water vapor estimated to be at least 140 trillion times that of all the water in Earth's oceans combined. The discovery of such an immense amount of water in such an early epoch of the universe provides crucial insights into the distribution of water in the cosmos and the conditions that prevailed in the early universe, suggesting that water was prevalent much earlier than previously thought.

The Multiverse Theory

The Multiverse Theory posits that our universe might be just one of countless others, each potentially governed by different physical laws and constants. This intriguing concept arises from the implications of quantum mechanics and inflationary cosmology, suggesting that every possible historical event is played out in alternate timelines in different universes. This theory not only challenges our understanding of reality but also expands the scope of possibility, encompassing universes where the fundamental aspects of nature, like gravity or electromagnetic force, could vary dramatically, leading to radically different forms of matter and energy.

The Cosmic Microwave Background

The Cosmic Microwave Background (CMB) is the afterglow radiation left over from the Big Bang, permeating the entire universe. First accidentally discovered in 1964 by Arno Penzias and Robert Wilson, the CMB provides a snapshot of the universe when it was just 380,000 years old, now cooled to a mere 2.7 degrees above absolute zero. This ancient light, which appears as a uniform glow across the sky in microwave frequencies, contains slight fluctuations that map the earliest large-scale structures of the universe. The study of the CMB has been pivotal in confirming the Big Bang theory and shaping our understanding of the universe's development.

The Age of the Universe

The age of the universe is currently estimated to be about 13.8 billion years, a calculation derived primarily from measurements of the Cosmic Microwave Background (CMB) and the expansion rate of the universe, known as the Hubble constant. This figure is based on highly precise observations made by the Planck satellite and other telescopes, which analyze the distance and speed of galaxies moving away from each other. These measurements allow astronomers to backtrack the expansion to the point of the Big Bang, giving us a remarkably accurate estimate of the universe's age.

Neutron Star Density

Neutron stars, the remnants of massive stars that have undergone supernova explosions, are among the densest objects in the universe. A typical neutron star has a mass about 1.4 times that of the Sun but is only about 20 kilometers in diameter. This extreme density means that a sugar-cube-sized amount of neutron star material would weigh about a billion tons on Earth. The intense gravitational field resulting from such density is powerful enough that even light struggles to escape, making neutron stars fascinating subjects for studying the laws of physics under extreme conditions.

The Pillars of Creation

The Pillars of Creation, iconic features within the Eagle Nebula, are towering columns of interstellar gas and dust located about 7,000 light-years from Earth. These structures are named for their role in star formation, as they contain several dense knots of gas that are in the process of collapsing under their own gravitational force to form new stars. Captured famously by the Hubble Space Telescope in 1995, these images not only provide a visually stunning glimpse into the process of star birth but also highlight the dynamic and evolving nature of the universe.

Supermassive Black Holes

Supermassive black holes, often found at the centers of massive galaxies, including our own Milky Way, are colossal in size, with masses that can range from hundreds of thousands to billions of times the mass of the Sun. These black holes play a critical role in the formation and evolution of galaxies. The energy released by material falling into the supermassive black hole can outshine the combined light of all the stars in the galaxy, creating what is known as a quasar, one of the brightest objects in the universe. This dynamic interaction highlights the influence these massive objects have on their surrounding environments, driving many of the processes that shape the observable universe.

The Accelerating Universe

The discovery that the universe is accelerating in its expansion was a groundbreaking revelation in modern cosmology, first observed in the late 1990s through studies of distant supernovae. This acceleration implies the presence of a mysterious force dubbed "dark energy," which constitutes about 68% of the total energy in the observable universe and acts against the pull of gravity on cosmic scales. This finding was so unexpected and profound that it led to the 2011 Nobel Prize in Physics, fundamentally altering our understanding of the cosmos and its ultimate fate.

Galactic Superclusters

Galactic superclusters are some of the largest structures in the universe, consisting of groups of galaxy clusters interconnected by filaments of galaxies and dark matter. One notable example is the Laniakea Supercluster, which includes our own Milky Way galaxy among over 100,000 other galaxies spread across about 500 million light-years. These immense structures are not just staggering in scale; they also trace the cosmic web that defines the large-scale structure of the universe, driven by the gravitational forces of dark matter. Understanding superclusters helps astronomers map the distribution and movement of galaxies across cosmic timescales.

Quantum Entanglement in Space

Quantum entanglement in space involves an intriguing phenomenon where pairs or groups of particles interact in such a way that the state of one particle instantaneously influences the state of the other, regardless of the distance separating them. This principle was dramatically demonstrated in a landmark experiment conducted by scientists using the Chinese satellite Micius in 2017, where particles were entangled over a record-breaking distance of more than 1,200 kilometers. This experiment not only confirmed quantum entanglement over vast distances but also paved the way for developing space-based quantum communication networks, potentially leading to highly secure, quantum-enabled communication systems.

The Color of the Universe

The color of the universe, often referred to as "cosmic latte," is the average color derived from the light of all the galaxies in the universe. This term and the associated color were coined in 2002 by a team of astronomers from Johns Hopkins University. They analyzed the spectral range of light from over 200,000 galaxies and adjusted for the effects of redshift and the universe's expansion. The result is a beige-white shade, suggesting that the universe's vast array of starlight and galactic energy blends into a relatively uniform color when viewed on a cosmic scale. This finding provides a visual summary of the universe's electromagnetic spectrum from billions of light-years away.

The Largest Volcano in the Solar System

Olympus Mons on Mars holds the title of the largest volcano in the solar system. Standing at about 22 kilometers (13.6 miles) high and spanning approximately 600 kilometers (373 miles) in diameter, it dwarfs any terrestrial volcano. Olympus Mons is a shield volcano, similar to those that form the Hawaiian Islands, but on a much larger scale. Its immense size is due in part to Mars' lower surface gravity, which allows geological structures to grow taller without collapsing under their own weight. This Martian giant's last eruption is estimated to have occurred around 25 million years ago, yet it remains a towering figure on the Martian landscape.

The Speed of Light

The speed of light in a vacuum is precisely 299,792 kilometers per second (approximately 186,282 miles per second), a fundamental constant in physics known as "c." This speed is the cosmic speed limit, the maximum speed at which all energy, matter, and information in the universe can travel. The constancy of the speed of light underpins many aspects of modern physics, including the theories of special and general relativity. It determines how we understand the structure of space-time and the flow of time itself, affecting everything from GPS satellite navigation to our understanding of the distances between stars and galaxies.

Galactic Winds

Galactic winds are powerful outflows of gas driven by the energy released from stars and supernovae within galaxies. These winds can travel at millions of kilometers per hour and are capable of carrying a substantial amount of material away from the galactic disk. Galactic winds play a crucial role in galaxy evolution by regulating the rate of star formation and contributing to the chemical enrichment of the intergalactic medium. They can be so forceful that they strip a galaxy of its interstellar medium, effectively quenching its ability to form new stars and altering its development. This dynamic process is pivotal in shaping the observable characteristics and lifecycle of galaxies across the universe.

WISE 0855-0714 The Coldest Star

WISE 0855-0714 is one of the coldest known objects in space outside our solar system, discovered by NASA's Wide-field Infrared Survey Explorer (WISE) telescope. This brown dwarf, located approximately 7.2 light-years away from Earth, has a temperature of about -48 to -13 degrees Celsius (-54 to 9 degrees Fahrenheit). With such frigid temperatures, WISE 0855-0714 is closer to the Earth's climate than to typical stars, and it is only slightly warmer than Jupiter, despite being in interstellar space. Its discovery adds important data to our understanding of atmospheric conditions and potential weather patterns on bodies beyond our solar system.

Cosmic Rays from Beyond the Galaxy

Cosmic rays are high-energy particles that travel through space at nearly the speed of light, originating from beyond our galaxy. Most cosmic rays are atomic nuclei stripped of their electrons, with a small fraction being solitary protons or heavier nuclei. Interestingly, some cosmic rays detected on Earth have energies exceeding what is achievable in the most powerful particle accelerators, such as the Large Hadron Collider. These ultra-high-energy cosmic rays are believed to be produced by some of the most cataclysmic events in the universe, such as supernovae, gamma-ray bursts, or the vicinity of black holes, challenging scientists to unravel their mysterious origins and propagation through space.

OJ 287: The Largest Black Hole

The largest known black hole, located in the galaxy OJ 287, boasts a mass approximately 18 billion times that of our Sun. This supermassive black hole stands out not only for its immense size but also because it is part of a binary black hole system, with a smaller companion black hole orbiting it. This unique pair provides a rare opportunity for scientists to study the dynamics and gravitational effects of such massive objects interacting closely. The behavior and trajectory of the companion black hole, as it orbits and occasionally passes through the accretion disk of the larger black hole, have been invaluable in testing predictions of general relativity.

The Boötes Void: A Galactic Mystery

The Boötes Void, also known as the Great Void, is one of the largest-known voids in the universe, located in the constellation Boötes. This immense expanse of space is about 330 million light-years in diameter and contains very few galaxies, only about 60 have been identified in a region where thousands would be expected. Discovered in 1981, the Boötes Void is a striking example of the large-scale structure of the universe, which includes vast empty spaces between filaments of galaxies. The origins and nature of these voids remain a significant puzzle in cosmology, challenging theories about the distribution of matter in the universe.

NGC 6302: The Butterfly Nebula

The Butterfly Nebula, also known as NGC 6302, is one of the most complex and intensely studied planetary nebulas known to astronomers. Located roughly 3,800 light-years away in the constellation Scorpius, it showcases a striking bipolar shape that resembles the wings of a butterfly. This spectacular appearance is caused by gas at more than 20,000 degrees Celsius being ejected by the central star at speeds exceeding 600,000 kilometers per hour. The star at the heart of the nebula, one of the hottest known, has a surface temperature of about 250,000 degrees Celsius, contributing to the nebula's vivid colors and dramatic wing-like structure.

IC 1101: The Largest Galaxy

IC 1101 is an elliptical galaxy recognized as one of the largest known galaxies in the observable universe. Situated over a billion light-years away, it resides at the center of the Abell 2029 galaxy cluster. IC 1101's immense size is truly staggering, with a diameter of approximately 6 million light-years, which is more than 50 times the size of the Milky Way. Its vast halo of stars and deep gravitational influence reflect its role as a dominant structure within its cluster, shaping the dynamics and evolution of its neighboring galaxies.

PSR J1748-2446ad: The Fastest Rotating Object

PSR J1748-2446ad is a neutron star that holds the record for the fastest-rotating celestial object discovered to date. Located approximately 18,000 light-years from Earth in the constellation Sagittarius, this pulsar spins at a staggering rate of 716 rotations per second. This high rotation speed means that the neutron star's surface at its equator is moving at nearly a quarter of the speed of light. The extreme conditions of PSR J1748-2446ad, including its rapid spin and strong magnetic field, provide a unique laboratory for studying the physics of matter under the most extreme pressures and densities known in the universe.

The Cosmic Calendar

The Cosmic Calendar is a method popularized by astronomer Carl Sagan to visualize the 13.8 billion-year history of the universe scaled down to a single year. In this framework, the Big Bang occurs at the stroke of midnight on January 1st, and the current moment marks the end of December 31st. Notably, all of recorded history fits into the last few seconds before midnight on New Year's Eve, illustrating just how brief the human chapter in the cosmic story has been. This perspective underscores the immense scale of cosmic time compared to human history, highlighting the fleeting nature of our existence in the universe.

Segue 2: The Faintest Galaxy

Segue 2 is notable for being one of the faintest galaxies known, located about 114,000 light-years away in the constellation Aries. Discovered as part of the Sloan Digital Sky Survey, this galaxy consists of only about 1,000 stars with a combined luminosity barely 900 times that of our sun, dimmer than some individual stars in our own galaxy. Segue 2's small size and low brightness make it a significant point of interest because it challenges traditional notions of what constitutes a galaxy, especially given its minimal star formation and weak gravitational pull.

The Hubble Ultra-Deep Field

The Hubble Ultra-Deep Field (HUDF) is an image of a small region of space in the constellation Fornax, created using Hubble Space Telescope data collected over several years. This image is remarkable for capturing about 10,000 galaxies, including some that are among the youngest and most distant known, appearing as they did just a few hundred million years after the Big Bang. This deep field view, which covers a speck of the sky only about the size of a tennis ball at 100 meters away, provides a profound glimpse into the universe's past, showcasing the evolving nature of galaxies over billions of years.

The Andromeda-Milky Way Collision

The Andromeda Galaxy and the Milky Way are on a collision course, with an expected convergence in approximately 4.5 billion years. This monumental event, often referred to as a galactic merger, will not resemble a typical collision due to the vast distances between stars within each galaxy. Instead of a destructive impact, the galaxies will gradually intertwine and merge over millions of years, eventually forming a single, larger elliptical galaxy. This process will dramatically change the night sky as viewed from Earth and will reshape the structure and dynamics of both galaxies.

UY Scuti: The Largest Star

UY Scuti is recognized as one of the largest known stars in the universe, situated approximately 9,500 light-years away in the constellation Scutum. With a radius about 1,700 times larger than the sun, if UY Scuti were placed at the center of our solar system, it would engulf the orbits of Mercury, Venus, Earth, Mars, and possibly even Jupiter. This immense size makes UY Scuti a prime example of a red supergiant, a star that has expanded enormously as it exhausts the nuclear fuel at its core. Its vast dimensions offer insights into the life cycle of massive stars and the processes that lead to their eventual demise as supernovae.

KIC 8462852: Tabby's Star

KIC 8462852, also known as Tabby's Star, is a star famous for its unusual and significant fluctuations in brightness. Unlike other stars with slight periodic dimming due to planets or debris passing in front, Tabby's Star has exhibited erratic dips in brightness by up to 22%, which is far more than can be caused by a planet. Discovered with data from the Kepler Space Telescope, this peculiar behavior has led to various theories about its cause, including swarms of comets, wrecked planets, and even speculative ideas involving alien megastructures. This star continues to be a subject of intense study and speculation within the astronomical community.

EBLM J0555-57Ab: The Smallest Star

EBLM J0555-57Ab is one of the smallest stars known, with a size just slightly larger than Saturn. Located about 600 light-years away, this star challenges the lower limits of how small a star can be while still enabling the fusion of hydrogen into helium in its core, a critical process for a celestial body to be considered a star. With a mass just sufficient to initiate nuclear fusion, EBLM J0555-57Ab provides valuable data for astronomers studying the boundary between the smallest stars and the largest gas giants, a distinction that is crucial for understanding the diversity of objects in the universe.

The Space Roar

The "space roar" is an unexpected and intense noise detected by NASA's ARCADE (Absolute Radiometer for Cosmology, Astrophysics, and Diffuse Emission) instrument in 2006. This phenomenon, which emanates from outside the Milky Way, is about six times louder than expected from known sources of radio waves in the universe, such as distant galaxies. The roar is not sound as we perceive it but a powerful radio signal whose origin remains a mystery, puzzling astronomers. Its detection has challenged existing theories about the origin and composition of radio backgrounds and continues to be a focus for further investigation in cosmology.

The Cosmic Distance Ladder

The Cosmic Distance Ladder is a series of methods by which astronomers determine the distances to celestial objects. This multi-step approach starts with more direct measurements for nearby objects and progressively moves to more indirect techniques for distant galaxies. The first rung includes parallax measurements for stars within a few hundred light-years. Subsequent methods involve standard candles like Cepheid variables for measuring distances within our galaxy and nearby galaxies, and Type Ia supernovae for distances to faraway galaxies. Each method builds upon the accuracy of the previous, allowing astronomers to map the universe's vast scales. This foundational concept in cosmology is critical for understanding the universe's structure and expansion.

The Tidal Force of the Moon

The tidal force of the Moon plays a crucial role in shaping the Earth's natural rhythms, most notably by influencing the rise and fall of ocean tides. This gravitational pull not only moves vast amounts of water but also gradually slows Earth's rotation. As a result, the length of a day on Earth is lengthening by about 1.7 milliseconds per century. Moreover, the energy this process takes from Earth is transferred to the Moon, causing it to slowly drift away from Earth at a rate of about 3.8 centimeters per year. This subtle interplay between Earth and its moon showcases the dynamic and ever-changing nature of celestial mechanics.

The Surface of the Sun

The surface of the Sun, known as the photosphere, is a turbulent and dynamic layer where the sun's visible light is emitted. Interestingly, despite its immense energy output, the photosphere is relatively cooler compared to other parts of the sun, with temperatures averaging about 5,500 degrees Celsius (9,932 degrees Fahrenheit). This is starkly cooler than the Sun's core, which reaches temperatures over 15 million degrees Celsius. The photosphere's cooler temperature allows us to observe light without being overwhelmed by the more intense radiation produced at hotter, deeper layers.

The Oort Cloud

The Oort Cloud is a theoretical cloud of predominantly icy objects that is believed to surround the Sun at a distance of up to 100,000 astronomical units, far beyond the orbits of Pluto and the known edge of the Kuiper Belt. This distant cloud is thought to be the source of long-period comets that can take hundreds, thousands, or even millions of years to complete one orbit around the Sun. The Oort Cloud represents the most distant region of our solar system's gravitational influence, serving as a reservoir of material left over from the solar system's formation about 4.6 billion years ago.

The Alcubierre Warp Drive

The Alcubierre Warp Drive is a theoretical concept that proposes a method of faster-than-light travel, based on a solution to Einstein's field equations in general relativity. Proposed by physicist Miguel Alcubierre in 1994, the concept involves a spacecraft that could achieve superluminal speed by contracting space in front of it and expanding space behind it. This mechanism would theoretically allow the spacecraft to move through a "warp bubble," effectively transporting it faster than the speed of light relative to the space outside the bubble, without violating the physical principles that restrict objects within space-time from exceeding light speed.

HD 131399: The Triple Star System

HD 131399 is a remarkable triple star system located about 340 light-years from Earth in the constellation Centaurus. This system is unique due to its complex orbital dynamics and the presence of a directly imaged exoplanet, HD 131399Ab, which was thought to have an unusually wide and stable orbit within this multi-star system. Initially, astronomers believed that this planet orbited its primary star while the other two stars orbited each other at a greater distance, creating a mesmerizing celestial dance. However, later observations suggested that what was initially believed to be a stable exoplanet might actually be a background star, adding a layer of intrigue and complexity to the understanding of multi-star systems.

The Ice Volcanoes of Ceres

Ceres, the largest object in the asteroid belt between Mars and Jupiter, is home to an intriguing geological feature: ice volcanoes. Unlike the fiery volcanoes on Earth, these cryovolcanoes, or "ice volcanoes," erupt with a mixture of water ice, salts, and mud instead of molten rock. The most prominent of these is Ahuna Mons, a solitary mountain about 4 kilometers high and 20 kilometers wide. It stands as a testament to Ceres' geologically active past. These icy eruptions are thought to occur when internal heat melts the dwarf planet's icy mantle, pushing the slush-like substance through the crust and onto the surface, a fascinating glimpse into a different kind of volcanic activity beyond Earth.

The Largest Impact Crater

The largest known impact crater on Earth is the Vredefort crater in South Africa. Formed over 2 billion years ago when a massive asteroid struck the planet, this crater originally measured about 300 kilometers in diameter, although erosion and geological processes have since reduced its visible size. The Vredefort crater is significant not only for its size but also for its impact on the Earth's geology and natural history. It provides crucial evidence of the planet's violent impact history and has helped scientists understand more about the Earth's geological layers and the forces that have shaped its surface. The crater has been designated a UNESCO World Heritage site due to its scientific importance and unique geological features.

The Elusive Planet Nine

The elusive Planet Nine is a hypothetical planet in the outer region of our solar system, theorized based on unusual clustering patterns in the orbits of trans-Neptunian objects (TNOs) beyond Neptune. This unseen planet is suggested to be significantly massive, potentially about 10 times the mass of Earth, and could explain the gravitational effects influencing these distant objects. The existence of Planet Nine could potentially redefine our understanding of the solar system's dynamics and structure, adding a mysterious outer component to the familiar roster of planets. Despite extensive searches, this potential planet remains unobserved, fueling ongoing debates and research in the astronomical community.

Chapter Three

Bizarre Animal Behaviors

Dancing Birds: The Flamboyant Flamenco of Flamingos

Flamingos are known for their strikingly vibrant feathers and their unique "dancing" behavior, which is actually a form of social bonding and a prelude to mating rituals. These distinctive movements include synchronized twirling, head-raising, and wing displays, performed in large groups. The dance helps flamingos establish and maintain social bonds within the flock and is crucial for selecting a mating partner. This flamboyant display is not just captivating but also emphasizes the importance of complex social interactions in the animal kingdom.

Tool-Using Fish: The Ingenious Archerfish

The archerfish is renowned for its remarkable tool-using ability, which involves shooting jets of water at insects and other prey located above the water's surface. This small fish accurately spits water up to several feet with remarkable precision to knock prey into the water, showcasing not just physical skill but also an impressive cognitive ability to judge distance and refraction. This behavior illustrates a sophisticated level of problem-solving that challenges the traditional view of tool use and intelligence in the animal kingdom, typically associated with mammals and birds.

Suicidal Reproduction: The Explosive End of the Antechinus

The antechinus, a small mouse-like marsupial found in Australia, exhibits a rare and extreme form of reproductive behavior known as semelparity, where it mates so intensely that it dies shortly after. During the breeding season, which lasts for about two weeks, male antechinuses engage in non-stop mating sessions that can last up to 14 hours, driven by a surge in stress hormones. This frenetic activity leads to immune system collapse, infections, and ultimately death. This strategy ensures that the males expend all their energy in fathering as many offspring as possible in one single reproductive season, sacrificing their own survival for reproductive success.

Immortal Jellyfish: The Never-Ending Life Cycle of Turritopsis dohrnii

Turritopsis dohrnii, commonly known as the immortal jellyfish, possesses a unique ability to revert to its juvenile form after reaching adulthood, effectively allowing it to bypass death and begin its life cycle anew. When faced with stress or physical assault, this jellyfish can transform all of its existing cells into a younger state, a process known as transdifferentiation. This capability not only allows it to potentially live indefinitely under the right conditions but also makes it a subject of significant interest for scientific research into aging and regenerative medicine.

The Drunken Monkeys of St. Kitts

On the Caribbean island of St. Kitts, vervet monkeys have developed a peculiar relationship with alcohol. Originally brought to the island aboard slave ships during the 17th century, these monkeys have since been observed stealing cocktails from tourists. Researchers studying these behaviors found that, much like humans, the monkeys show a range of drinking habits from teetotalism to heavy drinking. Interestingly, their social structure influences their drinking patterns, with more socially dominant monkeys tending to drink more frequently. This unusual adaptation provides insights into the effects of alcohol consumption across different species and the social factors influencing it.

Zombie Ants: The Mind Control of Ophiocordyceps

Zombie ants are the result of a parasitic infection by the fungus *Ophiocordyceps unilateralis*, which manipulates the behavior of its ant host in a way that benefits the fungus's life cycle. The fungus infects the ant, takes over its central nervous system, and eventually compels the ant to climb vegetation and clamp onto the underside of a leaf or twig using its mandibles. This specific positioning, often at an optimal height and humidity for the fungus, allows the fungus to thrive and eventually sprout from the ant's body, releasing spores to infect new ants. This bizarre and precise manipulation showcases nature's complex interactions and the extreme measures some organisms take to reproduce.

The Solar-Powered Sea Slug: Elysia chlorotica

Elysia chlorotica, a remarkable sea slug, exhibits a rare form of kleptoplasty, which allows it to incorporate chloroplasts from the algae it consumes into its own cells. By harnessing these stolen chloroplasts, the slug can perform photosynthesis, effectively converting sunlight into energy, much like a plant. This process enables Elysia chlorotica to survive for months on photosynthesis alone, after consuming algae just once. The ability to sustain itself through solar power not only blurs the lines between animal and plant kingdoms but also highlights an extraordinary evolutionary adaptation for energy acquisition.

The Moonwalking Manakin Bird

The moonwalking manakin, specifically the red-capped manakin *Ceratopipra mentalis*, is famous for its unique courtship dance that remarkably resembles the famous moonwalk dance move. Found in the rainforests of Central and South America, male manakins use a smooth sliding motion along a branch, almost as if they are gliding backward, to attract females. This eye-catching display is part of a complex dance routine that also includes rapid wing flapping and striking body movements. The dance not only showcases the male's physical fitness but also his ability to hold a territory, both of which are key factors in the female's choice of mate.

The Self-Sacrificing Octopus Mother

The self-sacrificing behavior of the female octopus after laying eggs is one of the most extreme examples of maternal care in nature. Species such as the giant Pacific octopus devote themselves entirely to protecting their eggs, foregoing food during the incubation period. This vigilant care can last for several months, during which the mother continuously aerates and cleans the eggs, ensuring their survival against predators and disease. Once the eggs hatch, the mother's life cycle completes, and she typically dies shortly afterward, having exhausted her energy reserves. This sacrifice ensures the maximum survival rate for her offspring, underlining the profound impact of parental care on the next generation's success.

The Decorator Crab's Camouflage

Decorator crabs, a group of crab species known for their unique method of camouflage, actively adorn their shells with materials from their environment, such as seaweed, sponges, and other debris. They attach these items to their shells using hook-like structures on their bodies. This behavior not only helps them blend seamlessly into their surroundings to evade predators, but it also serves as a form of active defense by using stinging or foul-tasting materials that deter predators. This fascinating adaptation showcases an intricate balance between animal behavior and environmental interaction, illustrating a sophisticated method of survival in the natural world.

The Temperature-Dependent Sex of Sea Turtles

The sex of sea turtles is determined by the temperature at which their eggs are incubated in the sand, a phenomenon known as temperature-dependent sex determination (TSD). Specifically, warmer sand temperatures tend to produce more female hatchlings, while cooler temperatures generally result in more males. This adaptation is particularly intriguing as it means that the climate can directly influence the population dynamics of sea turtles. Given the impacts of global warming, understanding and monitoring these temperature thresholds has become critical for conservation efforts aimed at maintaining balanced sex ratios within vulnerable sea turtle populations.

The Bowerbird's Artistic Nests

Bowerbirds, native to Australia and New Guinea, are renowned for their unique courtship behavior, which involves building elaborate and decorative structures called bowers. These are not nests for raising chicks, but rather artistic displays created to attract mates. Male bowerbirds meticulously collect and arrange objects like shells, leaves, flowers, and even discarded plastic items, organizing them by color and size to decorate their bowers. Some species even paint the inside of their bowers using materials like crushed berries. The complexity and aesthetic appeal of these structures play a crucial role in the female's choice of mate, demonstrating a fascinating intersection of natural behavior and what might be considered an artistic sense in the animal kingdom.

The Blood-Sweating Hippopotamus

Despite the vivid imagery their name suggests, hippopotamuses do not actually sweat blood. However, they do secrete a red, oily fluid from their skin glands, which serves as both an effective moisturizer and a protection against sunburn. This secretion, often called "blood sweat," contains pigments that are red (hipposudoric acid) and orange (norhipposudoric acid) which also have antibacterial properties, helping to prevent infections in the wounds that hippos might sustain in their often aggressive interactions with each other. This unique natural sunscreen and antiseptic showcase the hippopotamus's adaptation to its aquatic and sunny habitat.

The Electric Navigation of the Platypus

The platypus, one of nature's most eccentric creatures, possesses an extraordinary sensory capability: electroreception. This unique feature allows the platypus to detect electric fields generated by the muscular contractions of its prey. Found in the skin of its bill, the electroreceptors are fine-tuned to sense minute electrical signals in the water, aiding the platypus in navigating murky rivers and lakes where visibility is low. This ability is especially crucial during hunting, as the platypus closes its eyes, ears, and nostrils underwater, relying almost entirely on electroreception to locate food like shrimps and small fish.

The Migratory Marathon of the Arctic Tern

The Arctic tern holds the record for the longest annual migration of any animal in the world. Each year, these remarkable birds embark on a journey that spans from their breeding grounds in the Arctic to the Antarctic and back, covering a distance of about 71,000 kilometers (44,000 miles). This extensive travel ensures that the Arctic tern sees two summers per year and more daylight than any other creature on the planet. Their epic journey is driven by their search for abundant feeding territories, which allows them to maximize breeding success and survival rates. This incredible endurance and navigational feat highlight the Arctic tern's extraordinary adaptation to long-distance flight.

The Cooperative Hunting of Harris's Hawks

Harris's Hawks are unique among raptors for their remarkable behavior of cooperative hunting, akin to the tactics used by wolf packs. Unlike most birds of prey that are solitary hunters, these hawks hunt in groups of two to six. This strategy allows them to target larger prey than they could manage on their own, such as jackrabbits and other substantial animals. During a hunt, some hawks will flush out the prey while others wait in ambush, showcasing an extraordinary level of coordination and social behavior rarely observed in bird species. This cooperative approach not only increases their hunting success rate but also reinforces social bonds within the group.

The Pufferfish's Deadly Defense

The pufferfish is renowned for its unique and highly effective defense mechanism: it can inflate its body to several times its normal size by rapidly ingesting water or air. This sudden enlargement is complemented by the presence of spines on its skin, which become more pronounced when the fish puffs up, deterring most predators. Additionally, pufferfish are among the most poisonous vertebrates in the world, containing tetrodotoxin, a toxin potent enough to be lethal. This combination of physical and chemical defenses makes the pufferfish a formidable creature, despite its often slow and clumsy swimming style.

The Regenerating Limbs of Axolotls

Axolotls, a type of salamander native to Mexico, possess an extraordinary capability to regenerate not just limbs but also other complex body parts, including their tails, heart tissues, and even portions of the brain. Unlike most vertebrates, axolotls can heal without scarring and can restore the exact structure and functionality of the lost or damaged body parts. This remarkable regenerative process involves the transformation of their existing cells into stem cells, which then multiply and develop into the necessary tissues. Scientists study axolotls extensively, hoping to unlock secrets that could lead to breakthroughs in regenerative medicine for humans.

The Peacock Spider's Colorful Courtship

The peacock spider, native to Australia, is famous for its vibrant courtship display, which combines visual spectacle and rhythmic dancing. The male spider, which is notably colorful, features an iridescent flap on its back that it raises and fans out much like a peacock's tail during mating rituals. This colorful display is complemented by a series of elaborate dances including leg waving and body vibrations to attract female attention. These performances not only have to impress potential mates, but also sufficiently convince them of the male's suitability, as failure can sometimes result in the male being eaten by the female instead. This complex behavior showcases one of the most visually and behaviorally sophisticated mating rituals in the arachnid world.

The Bioluminescent Communication of Fireflies

Fireflies, are famous for their bioluminescent communication, a form of signaling that is not just captivating but also serves critical biological functions. Each species of firefly has a unique light pattern that helps males and females identify suitable mates. The light, produced through a chemical reaction in their lower abdomen, allows them to attract partners, deter predators, and sometimes mimic other species to lure prey. This bioluminescent communication is an effective adaptation for mating and survival, occurring in dusk or nighttime settings where their luminosity can be most visible and impactful.

Bees That Cook Their Enemies

Japanese honeybees, *Apis cerana japonica*, exhibit a remarkable defensive technique known as "heat balling," where they can literally cook their enemies to defend their hive. When faced with a threat like the invasive hornet, a group of worker bees will surround the intruder and vibrate their flight muscles intensely, raising their body temperature. This concerted action increases the temperature at the core of the bee ball to around 46 degrees Celsius (115 degrees Fahrenheit), which is lethal to the hornet but tolerable for the bees. This method showcases an extraordinary collective defense mechanism, allowing bees to protect their colony against larger and more powerful predators.

The Kleptoparasitism of the Cuckoo Bird

The cuckoo bird is notorious for its kleptoparasitic behavior, particularly known for laying its eggs in the nests of other bird species. This deceptive strategy involves the cuckoo female removing one egg from a host's nest and replacing it with one of her own, often mimicking the appearance of the host's eggs to avoid detection. Once the cuckoo chick hatches, it instinctively pushes the other eggs or young birds out of the nest to monopolize the food supply provided by the unsuspecting foster parents. This survival tactic allows the cuckoo to outsource the energy-intensive process of raising its young while maximizing the survival chances of its offspring.

The Sand-Bathing Sparrows

Sand-bathing is a fascinating behavior observed in several sparrow species, among other birds. Instead of using water, these sparrows will frequently roll in and flutter through sand or dry dirt. This activity serves multiple purposes: it helps the birds maintain their feather health by absorbing excess oil and dislodging parasites. The sand particles act as an abrasive, effectively cleaning and preening their feathers, which is crucial for flight efficiency and insulation. Moreover, sand-bathing is often a social activity, suggesting it also plays a role in strengthening communal bonds within flocks.

The Tusk Jousting of Narwhals

Narwhals, often referred to as the "unicorns of the sea," engage in a striking behavior known as tusk jousting. This activity involves males using their long, spiral tusks, which is actually an elongated tooth, to tap and rub against each other. While it was once thought that these interactions were aggressive and related to dominance or mating rights, recent observations suggest that tusk jousting may also be a way for narwhals to communicate and maintain social relationships within their pods. The tusks are highly innervated and sensitive, which supports the theory that they could be used to convey information about water properties or individual well-being during these interactions.

The Venomous Bite of the Slow Loris

The slow loris is one of the few mammals known to have a venomous bite, a rare trait among primates. This small, nocturnal creature produces venom in glands located on the inside of its elbows, which it combines with saliva when it bites. The venom can cause severe pain, swelling, and even anaphylactic shock in humans and is used primarily as a defense mechanism against predators. Interestingly, slow lorises also apply this venom to their fur while grooming, which acts as a deterrent to predators and provides protection to their offspring. This unique adaptation highlights the diverse evolutionary strategies animals have developed for survival.

The Aerial Acrobatics of Flying Fish

Flying fish, known for their dazzling aerial maneuvers, have evolved unique pectoral fins that enable them to leap out of the water and glide through the air. These fins, which are unusually large compared to those of other fish, act like wings, allowing flying fish to escape predators by making powerful, self-propelled leaps. During these flights, they can reach speeds over 35 miles per hour and cover distances exceeding 200 meters. The ability to glide is enhanced by their streamlined bodies that minimize air resistance, showcasing a remarkable adaptation to their oceanic environments.

The Huddling for Warmth in Emperor Penguins

Emperor penguins exhibit a remarkable survival behavior known as huddling, which is crucial during Antarctica's harsh winter. To conserve heat and shield themselves from extreme cold and wind, these penguins cluster tightly together, forming large groups that can include thousands of individuals. This strategy allows them to maintain a warmer microclimate at the center of the huddle. Remarkably, penguins take turns moving to the huddle's warmer interior and cooler exterior, ensuring that each member can warm up without monopolizing the most protected spots. This cooperative behavior is a key factor in their ability to survive and reproduce in one of Earth's most extreme environments.

The Bubble Net Feeding of Humpback Whales

Humpback whales engage in a unique and strategic feeding method known as bubble net feeding, which showcases their complex social behaviors and intelligence. This technique involves one or several whales swimming in a circle and blowing bubbles beneath a school of fish. The rising bubbles form a cylindrical "net" that traps the fish, confusing and concentrating them. As the fish cluster tightly together, the whales then swim upward through the "net" with their mouths open, engulfing thousands of fish in a single gulp. This cooperative feeding behavior not only maximizes their feeding efficiency but also highlights the advanced communication and coordination among humpback whales.

The Death Feigning of the Opossum

The opossum, a marsupial native to the Americas, is famously known for its behavior of playing dead when threatened, a tactic referred to as "playing possum." This involuntary reaction is a defense mechanism that involves the opossum falling to the ground, becoming stiff, closing its eyes, and even sticking out its tongue, sometimes accompanied by the release of a foul-smelling fluid from its anal glands. This act of feigning death can last from a few minutes to several hours, effectively convincing predators that it is not a viable meal. This response is triggered by extreme stress and serves as a last-ditch effort to deter predators when escape is not possible.

The Protective Mimicry of the Viceroy Butterfly

The viceroy butterfly is a notable example of protective mimicry, where it closely resembles the monarch butterfly, a species known for its toxicity to predators. For many years, it was believed that the viceroy mimicked the monarch's appearance to benefit from the monarch's reputation among predators who avoid the unpleasant taste and potential toxicity of the monarchs. However, more recent studies have shown that viceroys are also unpalatable, possessing their own form of chemical defense. This discovery has led to a new understanding that the viceroy's mimicry may be a case of Müllerian mimicry, where two harmful species mimic each other's warning signals to enhance predator avoidance.

The Antifreeze Proteins of Antarctic Fish

Antarctic fish, such as the Antarctic notothenioid, have developed a remarkable biological adaptation that allows them to survive in the icy waters of the Southern Ocean. These fish possess antifreeze proteins in their blood that prevent their body fluids from freezing despite temperatures that frequently drop below the freezing point of freshwater. The proteins work by binding to ice crystals that form within their bodies, inhibiting the crystals' growth and preventing them from becoming large enough to cause damage. This unique adaptation is essential for their survival in one of Earth's most extreme marine environments, enabling these fish to thrive where few other species can.

The Altruistic Behavior of African Wild Dogs

African wild dogs exhibit an impressive level of altruistic behavior within their packs, which is key to their survival. Known for their highly social nature, these dogs take care of the ill, old, and injured members by regurgitating food for those who cannot participate in hunts. Furthermore, in a pack, not all members may join the hunt; some stay behind to guard the pups. This cooperative dynamic extends to ensuring that the young eat first after a kill, which is unusual among carnivorous animals. Such behaviors underscore the complex social structures of African wild dogs and their reliance on teamwork, which is essential for maintaining strong, healthy packs.

The Magnetic Navigation of Sea Turtles

Sea turtles exhibit a remarkable navigational ability that is believed to be influenced by the Earth's magnetic fields. Throughout their long oceanic migrations, they can detect variations in the Earth's magnetic field and use this information to orient themselves and navigate across vast distances. This magnetic sense helps them return to the same beach where they were born, decades later, to lay their eggs. Research suggests that sea turtles may have a form of magnetic 'imprinting' that occurs early in life, enabling them to remember the specific magnetic signature of their natal beach, which guides them home despite years of travel across open oceans. This innate geomagnetic navigation underscores the deep connection between biological systems and planetary phenomena.

The Spit-Washing of Capuchin Monkeys

Capuchin monkeys, known for their intelligence and resourcefulness, engage in a unique behavior known as spit-washing. This involves the monkey rubbing saliva into its fur after thoroughly licking its hands and feet. While initially believed to be merely a grooming activity, further observations suggest that this behavior may serve multiple purposes, including cleaning and cooling their bodies. More interestingly, it is hypothesized that spit-washing could help the monkeys manage parasites and other skin irritations, indicating a rudimentary form of self-medication. This behavior highlights the complex and adaptive strategies capuchin monkeys use to maintain hygiene and health in their natural habitats.

The Echolocation of Bats

Bats are renowned for their use of echolocation, a sophisticated biological sonar system that enables them to navigate and hunt in total darkness. This ability involves emitting high-frequency sound waves from their mouths or noses, which bounce off objects in their environment and return as echoes. By interpreting these echoes, bats can construct detailed maps of their surroundings, detect obstacles, locate prey, and even discern the texture and density of objects, all in complete darkness. Echolocation is so precise that bats can detect insects as small as mosquitoes and skillfully maneuver through intricate spaces without colliding with obstacles. This remarkable sensory capability demonstrates one of the most refined adaptations in the animal kingdom for acoustic perception.

The Egg-Eating Habits of *Dasypeltis scabra*

The egg-eating snake, a unique species found primarily in Africa, has evolved a highly specialized diet exclusively consisting of bird eggs, unlike most other snakes that consume a more varied diet. These snakes are adept at consuming eggs much larger than their heads thanks to their flexible jaws and neck. Remarkably, after swallowing an egg whole, the snake uses bony vertebral protrusions inside its spine to crack the egg open. It then squeezes out the contents to consume, and finally regurgitates the empty eggshell. This adaptation allows them to extract maximum nutritional value without the need for venom or constricting abilities, showcasing an extraordinary example of evolutionary specialization.

The Honey-Gathering Skills of the Honeyguide Bird

The honeyguide bird, native to Africa, has an extraordinary symbiotic relationship with humans, where it leads them to beehives. The bird attracts the attention of humans with its distinctive calls and then flies toward a hive. Once the humans break open the hive and take the honey, the honeyguide feasts on the remaining beeswax and larvae, which are inaccessible without human intervention. This remarkable interaction not only demonstrates the bird's unique ability to communicate with another species but also illustrates an unusual mutualistic relationship in nature, where both species benefit directly from each other's actions.

The Beachcombing of the Pallas's Cat

The Pallas's cat, a small wild cat native to the grasslands and montane steppes of Central Asia, exhibits a curious behavior known as "beachcombing." This term describes how the cat walks with a flat-footed gait and its body held close to the ground, which is quite distinct from the more tiptoed stance typical of most cats. This peculiar walking style is thought to help the Pallas's cat remain less detectable to prey on the open plains where little cover is available. This adaptation enhances its stealth, making it a more effective hunter in its harsh, exposed habitat.

The Nut-Cracking Intelligence of Chimpanzees

Chimpanzees demonstrate remarkable intelligence and problem-solving abilities, particularly evident in their use of tools to crack nuts. In regions like West Africa, chimpanzees have been observed placing hard-shelled nuts on a stable surface and smashing them with a stone or heavy branch. This behavior not only requires the understanding and manipulation of tools but also involves the ability to choose the right type of stone and exert an appropriate amount of force to crack the nut without pulverizing it. Such sophisticated use of tools highlights their cognitive abilities, which are among the most advanced in the animal kingdom, reflecting complex thinking and planning skills.

Male Sea Horses Give Birth

Male seahorses have a unique reproductive role in the animal kingdom. Unlike most species, it is the male seahorse that becomes pregnant. The female deposits her eggs into a specialized brood pouch on the male's abdomen, where he fertilizes them. The male then carries the eggs in his pouch until they hatch, eventually giving birth to fully formed, miniature seahorses. This extraordinary process ensures that seahorse fathers take on the nurturing role, showcasing a rare example of male pregnancy.

The Playful Sliding of Otters

Otters are well-known for their playful behavior, particularly their habit of sliding down wet mud or snowbanks, which is both a mode of transportation and a form of play. This sliding not only conserves energy during travel but also appears to be genuinely enjoyable for the otters. They often climb back up the slope to slide down again, engaging in this activity repeatedly. This behavior, observed in both wild and captive otters, highlights their intelligence and their capacity for joy and playfulness, which play crucial roles in social bonding and learning within their groups.

The Camouflaging Cuttlefish

The cuttlefish is a master of camouflage, possessing the extraordinary ability to change both the color and texture of its skin in an instant. This adaptation helps it evade predators, ambush prey, and communicate with other cuttlefish. Its skin contains thousands of color-changing cells called chromatophores, which expand and contract to display different colors. Additionally, cuttlefish can alter their skin's texture to mimic their surroundings, such as appearing bumpy to blend in with coral. This remarkable ability is not just for concealment; it's also used during courtship displays and to intimidate rivals, showcasing their complex behavior and sophisticated control over their appearance.

The Thermal Soaring of Vultures

Vultures excel in a flying technique known as thermal soaring, which allows them to travel long distances while expending minimal energy. They achieve this by using rising currents of warm air, or thermals, generated from the sun heating the Earth's surface. Vultures can ascend to remarkable heights by circling within these thermals, then glide for miles to the next rising column of air without flapping their wings. This efficient method of travel is crucial for scavenging, as it enables them to cover vast areas in search of food with little effort, demonstrating a remarkable adaptation to their ecological niche.

The Water-Walking of the Basilisk Lizard

The basilisk lizard, often called the "Jesus Christ lizard," has the extraordinary ability to walk on water, a capability that helps it escape from predators. This ability is facilitated by the lizard's unique foot structure and rapid stride. The basilisk has long toes on its rear feet with fringes of skin that unfurl in the water, increasing surface area. When the lizard runs rapidly, it slaps its feet hard against the water, creating a tiny air pocket that keeps it from sinking, provided it maintains its speed. This fascinating adaptation allows the basilisk to sprint approximately 5 meters across water surfaces before needing to swim.

The Leaf-Mimicking Behavior of the Leaf-Tailed Gecko

The leaf-tailed gecko, native to Madagascar, exhibits an incredible form of camouflage known as leaf mimicry. This reptile has a flattened, leaf-shaped tail and a body color that can resemble the bark or leaves of its forest habitat. This adaptation allows it to blend seamlessly into its surroundings, making it nearly invisible to predators and prey alike. When threatened, the gecko can flatten its body against tree trunks, enhancing this effect, and if further threatened, it can shed its tail to escape, leaving the predator with only the detached tail. This exceptional camouflage not only provides effective protection but also makes the leaf-tailed gecko one of nature's most striking examples of evolutionary adaptation.

The Ant Rafts of Floods

During floods, fire ants display a remarkable survival strategy by forming large, floating rafts made entirely of their own bodies. When rising water threatens their colonies, these ants rapidly link together, using their jaws, legs, and sticky pads on their feet to create a waterproof raft. The structure is highly buoyant, allowing the entire colony, including the queen and larvae, to safely float on the water's surface until they reach dry land. This cooperative behavior not only exemplifies the ants' social organization but also their ability to adapt quickly to sudden environmental changes, ensuring the survival of the colony under extreme conditions.

The Vocal Mimicry of the Lyrebird

The lyrebird, native to Australia, is renowned for its incredible ability to mimic natural and artificial sounds from its environment. These birds can replicate almost any sound they hear, including chainsaws, car alarms, camera shutters, and the calls of other birds. Male lyrebirds use this unique skill to create complex and convincing audio landscapes during their mating displays, aiming to attract females with their repertoire. This extraordinary vocal mimicry not only showcases their adaptability but also highlights their role in the ecosystem as natural recorders of environmental sounds.

The Bioluminescent Lures of Deep-Sea Anglerfish

Deep-sea anglerfish employ a fascinating bioluminescent strategy to hunt in the pitch-dark depths of the ocean. These fish have a fleshy growth protruding from their heads, known as an esca, which they use as a lure. The esca contains bioluminescent bacteria that emit a glowing light. In the profound darkness of their habitat, this light attracts curious prey towards the anglerfish. Once an unsuspecting creature draws close enough, the anglerfish snaps it up with its powerful jaws. This method of predation is a brilliant adaptation to the lightless environment where traditional hunting methods would be ineffective.

The Bipedal Running of the Ostrich

The ostrich is the world's largest bird and is distinguished not only by its size but also by its remarkable ability to run at speeds of up to about 70 kilometers per hour (43 miles per hour), making it the fastest two-legged animal in the world. This incredible speed is facilitated by its unique leg structure, which includes two-toed feet and powerful, long legs that allow for large strides and rapid acceleration. Ostriches use their wings as stabilizers to maintain balance while running, flapping them to help change direction swiftly. This adaptation is essential for escaping predators and navigating the open grasslands of their African habitat.

The Synchronized Courtship of Fiddler Crabs

Fiddler crabs are known for their vibrant and synchronized courtship rituals, which are crucial for attracting mates. During the mating season, male fiddler crabs, recognizable by their disproportionately large claw, perform a series of waving displays. This involves rhythmically moving their giant claw up and down to catch the attention of females. The synchronization of these movements across numerous males creates a visually captivating display that not only increases individual chances of mating success but also reduces the likelihood of being singled out by predators. This synchronized behavior highlights the complex social interactions and communication strategies within the fiddler crab species.

Chapter Four

Inventions Ahead of Their Time

The Antikythera Mechanism: The World's First Computer

The Antikythera Mechanism, discovered in a shipwreck off the Greek island of Antikythera in 1901, is an ancient Greek device that dates back to around 100 BC. It is considered the world's first known analog computer. This intricate device was used to predict astronomical positions and eclipses for calendrical and astrological purposes as well as the cycles of the Olympic Games. The mechanism, consisting of at least 30 meshing bronze gears, demonstrates remarkable engineering skills and a deep understanding of astronomical phenomena, showcasing the sophisticated technology of the ancient Greeks long before the advent of modern computational devices.

Hero of Alexandria's Steam Engine: An Ancient Power Source

Hero of Alexandria, an ancient Greek engineer and mathematician, invented the first known steam engine, called the aeolipile, around the 1st century AD. This device, also referred to as Hero's engine, consisted of a hollow sphere mounted on a water kettle. Steam produced by the kettle's boiling water escaped through two bent tubes on opposite sides of the sphere, causing it to spin rapidly. Although primarily considered a novelty or demonstration piece, Hero's aeolipile represents one of the earliest examples of converting steam power into rotary motion, laying foundational concepts for the development of modern steam engines centuries later.

The Baghdad Battery: A Possible Ancient Electric Cell

The Baghdad Battery, discovered in the 1930s near Baghdad, Iraq, is a fascinating artifact that dates back to the Parthian or Sassanid periods, around 250 BC to AD 224. This device consists of a clay jar containing a copper cylinder that encases an iron rod. The theory posits that when the jar was filled with an acidic or alkaline substance, it could have functioned as an electrochemical cell, possibly used for electroplating gold onto silver objects. While the exact purpose of the Baghdad Battery remains a topic of debate among archaeologists, its design suggests a knowledge of basic electrochemistry long before the modern development of electric cells.

Archimedes' Screw: An Ingenious Water Lifter

Archimedes' Screw, attributed to the ancient Greek mathematician Archimedes of Syracuse in the 3rd century BC, is a machine designed for raising water. The device consists of a screw inside a hollow pipe, turned by hand via a handle at the top. When the bottom end is placed in water and the screw is rotated, water is drawn up the spiral and out the top. This ingenious invention was initially used for irrigating fields and removing bilge water from ships. Its effectiveness and simplicity have stood the test of time, with variations of Archimedes' Screw still used today in modern industrial applications for moving liquids and granulated solids.

Da Vinci's Flying Machine: The Dream of Human Flight

Leonardo da Vinci's flying machine, sketched in the late 15th century, represents one of his many visionary ideas that presaged future inventions. His design, often called the "ornithopter," aimed to enable human flight by mimicking the wing-flapping of birds. The device featured large wings connected to a system of pulleys and gears, intended to be powered by the pilot's own muscle power. While never built or tested in his lifetime, da Vinci's detailed studies of bird flight and his conceptual blueprints laid foundational ideas for the later development of aviation, highlighting his extraordinary foresight and understanding of aerodynamics.

Da Vinci's Parachute

Leonardo da Vinci's parachute design, conceived in the early 16th century, stands as a testament to his ingenuity and quite possibly a lack of confidence in the flying machine. His concept, detailed in his Codex Atlanticus, features a pyramidal structure made from sealed linen cloth held open by a wooden frame, which he theorized could allow any man to "throw himself down from any great height without suffering any injury." Although da Vinci's design was never tested during his lifetime, its principles were sound enough that when a replica was constructed and tested in 2000, it successfully carried a brave skydiver safely to the ground, proving the design's effectiveness nearly 500 years after it was conceived.

The Roman Concrete: An Enduring Formula

Roman concrete, used extensively throughout the Roman Empire from around 300 BC to 476 AD, remains celebrated for its extraordinary durability and longevity. This ancient material was made from a mix of volcanic ash, lime (calcium oxide), and seawater, creating a chemical reaction that produced a material resistant to cracking and environmental wear. What sets Roman concrete apart from modern formulas is its ability to strengthen over time due to the incorporation of volcanic ash, which helps the concrete to resist degradation even in harsh marine environments. This enduring quality is why many Roman architectural marvels, like the Pantheon and aqueducts, have stood the test of time, still standing robust after millennia.

The Han Dynasty Seismoscope: An Early Earthquake Detector

The Han Dynasty seismoscope, invented by the Chinese astronomer and mathematician Zhang Heng in AD 132, is recognized as one of the earliest known devices for detecting earthquakes. This ingenious instrument, described as resembling a bronze vase, featured a pendulum inside that, when disturbed by seismic activity, would trigger a mechanism causing one of several dragon heads mounted on the vase to release a ball into the mouth of a corresponding frog at the base, indicating the direction of the earthquake. Zhang Heng's seismoscope was remarkably sensitive, reportedly capable of detecting earthquakes occurring hundreds of kilometers away, well before any perceptible shaking was felt at the location of the device itself.

The Dover Bronze Age Boat

The Dover Bronze Age Boat, discovered in 1992 during road construction in Dover, England, is one of Europe's oldest known seagoing vessels, dating back approximately 3,500 years to the Middle Bronze Age. Remarkably preserved, the boat was constructed using sophisticated woodworking techniques, including stitched planks and a unique form of waterproofing achieved through the use of moss and yew tree resin. This discovery highlights the period's advanced maritime technology and provides invaluable insights into the early trade and cultural exchange across the Channel between ancient Britain and mainland Europe. The boat's design and construction techniques reflect a deep understanding of seafaring, crucial for trade and communication in prehistoric times.

Leonardo da Vinci's Robot Knight

Leonardo da Vinci's Robot Knight, designed around 1495, is one of the earliest concepts of a humanoid automaton. According to da Vinci's sketches, this mechanical knight was designed to perform several human-like movements, including sitting up, moving its arms, and lifting its visor. Powered by a series of pulleys, gears, and cranks, this innovative design reflects da Vinci's advanced understanding of anatomy and engineering. The Robot Knight was intended to amuse and impress at courtly events, showcasing not only da Vinci's artistic creativity but also his prowess in mechanical design. This invention highlights the Renaissance's blend of art, science, and technology, foreshadowing modern robotics.

The South Pointing Chariot: An Ancient Compass on Wheels

The South Pointing Chariot, an ancient Chinese invention dating back to around the 3rd century BC, was a remarkable early form of non-magnetic, mechanical compass. Unlike magnetic compasses, which point towards the magnetic north, this ingenious device used differential gearing to maintain a fixed direction, usually south, regardless of the turns made by the chariot. This was achieved through a system where the turning of the wheels was mechanically linked to a figure or pointer that always indicated the same cardinal direction. This technology was not only a navigational aid but also symbolized technological prowess and divine guidance in ancient China, illustrating the advanced level of early Chinese engineering and scientific inquiry.

The Damascus Steel: A Lost Art of Swordmaking

Damascus steel, renowned for its strength, resilience, and distinctive flowing water patterns on the blade, was a highly sought-after material in the Middle Ages, primarily used for crafting swords and other bladed weapons. Originating from the Near East, the exact process and composition of the original Damascus steel became a lost art around the 18th century. The steel's legendary hardness and sharpness were attributed to the unique impurities in the metals used and the skilled forging techniques that created a complex crystalline structure. Modern metallurgists and blacksmiths have attempted to recreate the distinctive pattern and properties of Damascus steel, but the original manufacturing secrets remain a historical mystery.

Nikola Tesla's Remote Controlled Boat

In 1898, Nikola Tesla astounded the public by demonstrating a radio-controlled boat at Madison Square Garden. Using a small box, he wirelessly controlled the boat's movements in a pool, showcasing the groundbreaking potential of remote control technology. This early demonstration was far ahead of its time, anticipating the development of modern remote-operated devices and robotics. Tesla's innovation highlighted his extraordinary foresight and contributions to the field of wireless communication and control.

The Aeolian Harp: Harnessing the Wind's Music

The Aeolian harp is a fascinating musical instrument named after Aeolus, the ancient Greek god of the wind. Invented in the 17th century, it is designed to be played not by human hands, but by the natural movement of the wind. The harp is typically placed in a window where the wind can pass across its strings, producing harmonic sounds or tones that vary with the strength and direction of the wind. This creates an ethereal, continuously changing musical performance that is entirely governed by the weather conditions. The Aeolian harp was a popular fixture in the Romantic era, celebrated for its ability to turn the invisible force of the wind into audible and often hauntingly beautiful music.

The Mechanical Galleon: An Automaton of the Sea

The Mechanical Galleon is a remarkable automaton from the late Renaissance, crafted to mimic the appearance and function of a sailing ship. Designed as a table centerpiece for royal banquets, this intricate device not only resembled a galleon but also featured moving parts and figures, such as sailors that rowed, cannons that fired, and musicians that played. It was operated by an intricate system of gears and springs hidden within its hull. The Mechanical Galleon exemplifies the fascination with automata during the Renaissance, showcasing the period's blend of artistic creativity and mechanical engineering to create entertaining and sophisticated gadgets.

The Iron Pillar of Delhi: Rust-Resistant Marvel

The Iron Pillar of Delhi, standing in the Qutb complex in India, is a metallurgical marvel known for its remarkable resistance to corrosion, despite being over 1,600 years old. Made around A.D. 400, the pillar is composed of almost pure wrought iron and stands 7.3 meters high, weighing approximately 6 tons. The secret to its endurance lies in the high phosphorus content of the iron, which forms a protective layer of misawite, a compound of iron, oxygen, and hydrogen, on the surface. This thin layer has protected the pillar from significant rust over the centuries, making it a significant study subject for ancient Indian ironworking skills and corrosion resistance technology.

The Longyou Caves: A Monumental Ancient Engineering Feat

The Longyou Caves, located in Zhejiang province, China, are an enigmatic series of vast underground spaces that were hand-carved out of solid siltstone during the Eastern Han Dynasty around 2,000 years ago. Covering an area of 30,000 square meters with the largest cave exceeding 18 meters in height, these caverns were not discovered until 1992 when a local villager drained a pond revealing the hidden marvels beneath. Despite their grand scale and precision, there are no historical records of their construction, purpose, or even existence. This absence of documentation, along with the sheer labor required to excavate approximately 1,000,000 cubic meters of rock, makes the Longyou Caves one of the most mysterious and sophisticated ancient engineering feats in China.

The Nebra Sky Disk: A Bronze Age Cosmic Map

The Nebra Sky Disk, dating back approximately 3,600 years, is one of the oldest known depictions of the cosmos worldwide. Discovered in 1999 near Nebra, Germany, this bronze disk, about 30 centimeters in diameter, is adorned with gold leaf symbols that are interpreted as the sun, moon, and stars, including a cluster thought to represent the Pleiades. What makes the disk particularly significant is its use as a complex astronomical clock for the synchronization of the lunar and solar calendars. The Nebra Sky Disk's blend of astronomical precision and artistic craftsmanship provides a rare glimpse into the early knowledge and valuation of celestial events by Bronze Age societies in Europe.

Charles Babbage's Analytical Engine

Charles Babbage's Analytical Engine, conceived in the 1830s, is considered the first design for a general-purpose computer. Babbage, a British mathematician, philosopher, inventor, and mechanical engineer, designed the Analytical Engine to be programmable, a groundbreaking concept at the time. Unlike his earlier Difference Engine, which was intended to perform only a specific calculation, the Analytical Engine was capable of being programmed with punched cards, an idea borrowed from the Jacquard loom used for weaving complex patterns. Although it was never completed during his lifetime, Babbage's design laid the foundational principles of the modern computer, including the use of a stored program and separate storage and processing units.

The First Vending Machine

The first known vending machine was invented by the Greek engineer and mathematician Hero of Alexandria in the 1st century AD. This early device was created to dispense holy water in Egyptian temples. Upon inserting a coin into the machine, it would fall onto a pan attached to a lever, opening a valve that let out a modest flow of holy water. Once the coin was dislodged from the pan, the lever would snap back, and the valve would shut off. This clever use of simple mechanics not only regulated access to the water but also demonstrated early principles of automation and coin-operated service.

Chester Carlson's Revolutionary Breakthrough in Document Reproduction

In 1938, Chester Carlson developed the process of electrophotography, which he later named xerography. This invention, the foundation for modern photocopiers and laser printers, revolutionized document reproduction. Despite its significance, Carlson faced numerous rejections from companies before the Haloid Company (later Xerox Corporation) saw its potential in the late 1940s. Carlson's perseverance ultimately led to a technology that transformed office work and document management worldwide.

The Etruscan Tumulus Tombs: Engineering Wonders

The Etruscan tumulus tombs, primarily found in central Italy, are notable for their impressive engineering and architectural design, dating back to the Iron Age. These tombs consist of burial mounds built above ground in a circular plan and often covered with earth or stones, creating a dome-shaped structure known as a tumulus. The interiors of these mounds were intricately laid out with multiple burial chambers, resembling the homes in which the Etruscans once lived, complete with rooms and furniture carved from rock. This practice not only signifies the Etruscans' belief in an afterlife where the dead continued their earthly existence but also showcases their skill in stone carving and constructing enduring structures, some of which have preserved detailed wall paintings and artifacts for over two millennia.

The Dymaxion Car

The Dymaxion Car, designed by the visionary inventor Buckminster Fuller in the early 1930s, was a highly innovative vehicle that broke the conventional mold of car design. Its teardrop shape and three-wheel configuration, two front wheels and one rear wheel that steered, aimed to maximize efficiency and minimize resource use. The Dymaxion could seat up to eleven people and was capable of reaching speeds of up to 90 miles per hour, remarkable for its time. Despite its futuristic design and potential for revolutionizing transport, only three prototypes were ever built, partly due to a fatal crash during a demonstration that maligned its reputation for safety. The Dymaxion remains a symbol of ahead-of-its-time design thinking and Fuller's comprehensive approach to problem-solving.

The Zhengzhou Shang Dynasty Wall: An Ancient Defense System

The Zhengzhou Shang Dynasty Wall, dating back to around 1500 BCE, is one of the earliest examples of urban defense systems in ancient China. Located in what is now Henan province, this massive wall was constructed under the Shang dynasty to protect the city of Zhengzhou, which served as a capital during the dynasty's early period. The wall is notable for its scale and construction technique, having been made from stamped earth and layers of mud and gravel, a method known as "hangtu." This construction not only signifies the strategic importance of Zhengzhou but also reflects the advanced state of urban planning and military architecture in ancient China during the Bronze Age.

The Ctesibius Water Clock: A Hellenistic Timekeeper

The Ctesibius Water Clock, invented in the 3rd century BCE by the ancient Greek engineer Ctesibius of Alexandria, represents a significant advancement in timekeeping technology. Known as a clepsydra, this clock used the steady flow of water to measure time more accurately than previous sundials or earlier water clocks that did not regulate flow. Ctesibius' design included intricate gearwork and a float system that drove a mechanical dial to display the hours as the water level changed. This innovation not only improved the precision of time measurement, especially indoors and at night, but also showcased the sophistication of Hellenistic engineering and its contributions to later developments in mechanical devices.

The Abū Rayhān al-Bīrūnī Astrolabe: Precision in the Stars

Abū Rayhān al-Bīrūnī, a renowned scholar of the Islamic Golden Age, significantly advanced the field of astronomy with his refined astrolabes, around the early 11th century.

Al-Bīrūnī's astrolabes were highly precise instruments used for solving problems relating to time and the position of the sun and stars in the sky. These devices were critical for navigation and determining the times for prayer and the direction to Mecca for Muslims. Al-Bīrūnī's contributions included detailed mathematical treatments and corrections that improved the accuracy of these instruments, showcasing his mastery in integrating mathematics with practical astronomy. His work enhanced astrolabes' functionality and influenced astronomical studies across medieval Europe and the Islamic world.

The Sacsayhuamán Fortress: A Peruvian Architectural Marvel

The Sacsayhuamán Fortress, located on the outskirts of Cusco, Peru, is an architectural marvel of the Incan Empire, famous for its massive, tightly interlocking stones. Constructed in the 15th century, this fortress showcases the Incas' advanced dry stone wall technology, with some of the boulders used in the walls weighing as much as 200 tons. The precision with which these enormous stones were cut and fitted together is so exact that not even a blade of grass can be inserted into the joins. This precision, coupled with the walls' zigzagging design, was not only aesthetically pleasing but also provided a strategic military advantage, helping to protect the Incan capital against invasions. The engineering skills evident in Sacsayhuamán remain a testament to Incan builders' sophistication and their deep understanding of stone masonry.

The Roman Hypocaust: An Ancient Heating System

The Roman hypocaust was an innovative heating system developed during the Roman Empire, primarily used to heat bathhouses and wealthy homes. This ancient form of underfloor heating involved constructing a raised floor supported by pillars, beneath which hot air and smoke from a furnace would circulate. The heat generated would then rise, warming the floors and walls above. This system provided consistent heat during cooler seasons and demonstrated the Romans' advanced engineering capabilities and commitment to comfort and luxury. The hypocaust is a testament to the sophistication of Roman architectural technology, influencing modern heating practices.

The Jantar Mantar Observatory: Celestial Precision

The Jantar Mantar Observatory in Jaipur, India, constructed in the early 18th century by Maharaja Sawai Jai Singh II, is a collection of nineteen architectural astronomical instruments. The observatory features the world's largest stone sundial, known as the Samrat Yantra, which stands at a height of about 27 meters. This monumental instrument allows observations of astronomical positions with the naked eye and is accurate to within two seconds. The precision and scale of Jantar Mantar highlight the advanced astronomical knowledge and architectural ingenuity of the time, making it not only a pioneering scientific facility but also a UNESCO World Heritage site.

The Lycurgus Cup: A Nanotechnology Marvel

The Lycurgus Cup, a 4th-century Roman glass chalice, is a remarkable example of ancient nanotechnology. This artifact displays a fascinating optical phenomenon known as dichroic glass, which changes color depending on the light direction. When light shines from behind, the cup appears red, and when light is in front, it looks green. This effect is due to the presence of gold and silver nanoparticles in the glass, which were ground down to as small as 50 nanometers in diameter, roughly one-thousandth the size of a grain of table salt. The precise manipulation of these particles suggests a sophisticated understanding of materials, making the Lycurgus Cup one of the earliest known examples of nanotechnology in use.

Charles Townes' Visionary Concept for the Laser

In 1955, Charles Townes developed the concept for the laser, foreseeing its wide-ranging applications years before it became reality. His pioneering work laid the foundation for the first operational laser in 1960. This breakthrough technology has since transformed various fields, including medicine, telecommunications, entertainment, and manufacturing. Townes' vision and innovation paved the way for a tool that is now integral to numerous modern technologies.

The Automata of Al-Jazari: Mechanical Wonders

Al-Jazari, a 12th-century Muslim inventor from the Artuqid dynasty of Mesopotamia, is celebrated for his pioneering contributions to the field of engineering, particularly his work with automata. Among his most fascinating creations detailed in his book, "The Book of Knowledge of Ingenious Mechanical Devices," was a band of automated musicians on a boat, designed to entertain at royal parties. This mechanical ensemble operated via a complex arrangement of gears, levers, and floats driven by the flow of water. Al-Jazari's automata were not only marvels of artistic creativity but also showcased early uses of programmable logic and are considered precursors to modern robotics and mechanical engineering.

The Panjandrum

The Panjandrum was an experimental World War II weapon designed by the British military to breach heavily fortified German defenses along the coastlines. Introduced in 1943, this bizarre, self-propelled device consisted of two large, rocket-powered wheels attached to a central drum filled with explosives. The idea was for the Panjandrum to race across the beach, propelled by rockets, and detonate against enemy fortifications. However, during testing, the contraption proved to be highly unpredictable; it often veered off course and was prone to failure, as the rockets could detach or misfire. Despite its ingenious concept, the Panjandrum was never deployed in actual combat due to its erratic behavior and unreliability, ultimately earning a place in history as an eccentric example of wartime engineering.

The Great Zimbabwe Ruins: A Lost African Civilization

The Great Zimbabwe Ruins are the remnants of a sprawling stone city constructed between the 11th and 15th centuries in modern-day Zimbabwe. It was the capital of the Kingdom of Zimbabwe, which thrived during the country's Late Iron Age. The ruins' most impressive and recognizable structure is the Great Enclosure, featuring walls up to 11 meters high and extending over 250 meters, making it the largest ancient structure in sub-Saharan Africa. These walls were constructed using a method called dry stone architecture, involving meticulously cut stones that were stacked without the use of mortar. The site, which once housed up to 18,000 people, is notable not just for its architectural sophistication but also for its role as a major trading center, evidenced by artifacts found from as far afield as China and Persia.

The Airlift Pump of Vitruvius: Roman Engineering Ingenuity

The Airlift Pump of Vitruvius, devised by the ancient Roman engineer Vitruvius in the 1st century BCE, showcases Roman ingenuity in hydraulic engineering. This device, described in Vitruvius's treatise "De Architectura," was used to aerate water and remove contaminants from deep mine shafts. The pump operated on a principle where compressed air was introduced into a submerged pipe, decreasing the water's density inside the pipe and causing the water to rise above the surrounding water level. This clever use of basic pneumatic principles allowed the Romans to efficiently manage water in mining operations, illustrating their advanced understanding of both engineering and environmental management.

The Tiangong Kaiwu: An Encyclopedia of Chinese Technology

The "Tiangong Kaiwu," or "The Exploitation of the Works of Nature," is a comprehensive Chinese encyclopedia compiled by Song Yingxing in 1637 during the Ming Dynasty. This remarkable work is renowned for its detailed illustrations and descriptions of various technologies and processes used in agriculture, textile manufacturing, and various other crafts during Song's time. The encyclopedia covers a wide range of subjects, from the cultivation of silk worms to the extraction of soybean oil, reflecting an advanced level of technological understanding and application. Notably, Song Yingxing's work stands out for its empirical approach, as he emphasized direct observation and practical experience over theoretical knowledge, making it a valuable resource for understanding ancient Chinese technology and industry practices.

The Strasbourg Astronomical Clock: A Renaissance Masterpiece

The Strasbourg Astronomical Clock, located in the Cathedral of Notre-Dame in Strasbourg, France, is a Renaissance masterpiece that blends art, engineering, and astronomy. Built between 1838 and 1843, this is actually the third clock to adorn the cathedral, with the first dating back to the 14th century. The current clock features an intricate set of automata, including a rooster that crows, a parade of apostles that pass before Christ, and a celestial globe that tracks the real movements of the stars and planets. One of the most fascinating aspects is its orrery, which mechanically represents the Solar System, demonstrating not only the clockmaker's skill but also the scientific understanding of the era. This clock remains a symbol of human ingenuity and the rich intersection of science and art during the Renaissance.

The Mayan Calendar: Advanced Timekeeping

The Mayan Calendar, developed by the ancient Maya civilization of Central America, is renowned for its complexity and precision in astronomical and chronological measurement. It consisted of several cycles or counts of different lengths. The most famous of these is the Long Count, a linear calendar that tracked a cycle of 5,125.36 years, starting in 3114 BCE, which many misconstrued as predicting the end of the world in 2012. The Mayans also used a 260-day ceremonial calendar called the Tzolk'in, and a 365-day solar calendar called the Haab'. These calendars were used in conjunction to schedule ceremonial events, agricultural activities, and track celestial movements with remarkable accuracy, demonstrating the Mayans' sophisticated understanding of time and astronomy.

The Benin Bronzes: African Metalworking Mastery

The Benin Bronzes, a collection of intricately crafted sculptures and plaques from the Kingdom of Benin in modern-day Nigeria, are celebrated not only for their artistry but also for their historical significance. Created between the 13th and 19th centuries, these metal plaques were cast in bronze and brass using the sophisticated lost-wax casting technique. They adorned the royal palace of the Benin Kingdom, depicting a variety of scenes from courtly life, including images of warriors, dignitaries, and divine figures. The Benin Bronzes are considered one of the highest achievements of African metalworking and artistry, reflecting the culture, governance, and religion of the historic Benin Kingdom.

The Hero's Fountain: An Ancient Hydraulic Device

The Hero's Fountain, devised by the ancient Greek engineer Hero of Alexandria in the first century AD, is an ingenious example of early hydraulic and pneumatic science. This device uses principles of air and water pressure to create a continuous flow of water. Essentially, it consists of three interconnected vessels; when the bottom container is filled with water, the displaced air pushes water up through a tube into a higher vessel, which then cascades into a fountain display. Hero's invention not only entertained but also demonstrated fundamental principles of physics, showcasing the advanced understanding of mechanics possessed by scholars of the Hellenistic world.

The Nan Madol Ruins: A Pacific Engineering Feat

Nan Madol is an archaeological site on the eastern shore of the island of Pohnpei in Micronesia, renowned for its unique construction. Built approximately between 1200 and 1500 AD, it consists of nearly 100 artificial islets across a coral reef, constructed with logs of basalt and coral boulders. These massive stones, some weighing several tons, were transported from various parts of the island, a feat that still puzzles historians today. Known as the "Venice of the Pacific," Nan Madol was the ceremonial and political seat of the Saudeleur dynasty, reflecting sophisticated engineering skills and social organization long before European contact.

The Qin Shi Huang Mausoleum: An Army of Terracotta Warriors

The Qin Shi Huang Mausoleum, home to the famous Terracotta Army, houses over 8,000 life-sized clay soldiers, each uniquely crafted to guard the first Emperor of China, Qin Shi Huang, in his afterlife. Discovered in 1974 near Xi'an, China, these figures were buried in 210-209 BCE and are positioned according to rank, complete with horses, chariots, and weapons. This monumental project not only exemplifies the emperor's authority and the resources at his disposal but also provides a fascinating insight into the military practices, artistry, and religious beliefs of the time. The site remains one of the most significant archaeological finds, offering a window into ancient Chinese culture and the elaborate rites associated with the afterlife.

The Ktesibios Water Organ: Musical Hydraulics

The Ktesibios Water Organ, invented by the ancient Greek engineer Ktesibios in Alexandria in the 3rd century BC, is one of the earliest known keyboard instruments and a remarkable example of combining hydraulics with music. Unlike its predecessors, this innovative device used water to regulate air pressure in its pipes, producing a steady flow that allowed for clear and consistent sound output. The water organ's keys activated levers that opened valves, allowing air to pass through and create music. Ktesibios' creation was not only a technical marvel that influenced the development of later musical instruments, including the church organ, but also demonstrated the sophisticated application of physics and engineering in the Hellenistic world.

The Anemometer of Leon Battista Alberti: Measuring the Wind

Leon Battista Alberti, a Renaissance humanist and architect, invented the first known mechanical anemometer in 1450. This device was designed to measure wind speed, enhancing the understanding of weather patterns at the time. Alberti's anemometer consisted of a disk placed perpendicular to the wind direction, and its angle of tilt due to the wind was used to estimate wind speed based on a scale he developed. This invention not only marked a significant advance in meteorological instruments but also set the foundation for future developments in environmental science, illustrating the breadth of intellectual curiosity during the Renaissance.

The Floating Gardens of Tenochtitlan: Aztec Agriculture

The Floating Gardens of Tenochtitlan, known as "chinampas," were an ingenious agricultural technique used by the Aztecs to expand arable land in their capital city, located on what is now Mexico City. These man-made islands were created by staking out shallow lake beds and then layering soil, sediment, and decaying vegetation to form fertile plots. Surrounded by water, the chinampas were highly productive, allowing for several crop cycles per year, unlike traditional farming methods. This system not only supported the dense population of Tenochtitlan with a consistent and diverse food supply but also demonstrated the Aztecs' advanced understanding of sustainable agriculture and urban planning.

The Roman Mill: Water-Powered Sawmills

One of the most significant technological innovations of the ancient world was the introduction of water-powered sawmills by the Romans, particularly noted during the 3rd century AD. These early industrial machines were primarily used in the construction of large buildings and in the production of marble for monuments. The Roman mill featured a complex system where waterwheels powered saw blades, dramatically increasing productivity compared to manual labor. The most famous historical account comes from the Hierapolis sawmill in Asia Minor, which represents one of the earliest known applications of hydropower, predating the widespread use of water-driven machinery in the medieval period. This advancement not only improved efficiency in material processing but also showcased Roman engineering prowess in utilizing natural resources for mechanical purposes.

The Ancient Refrigerators: The Yakhchāls of Persia

The Yakhchāls of ancient Persia, dating back to as early as 400 BCE, were innovative structures used to store ice and food throughout the year, even in the desert regions during summers. These dome-shaped constructions, made from a unique insulation material consisting of sand, clay, egg whites, lime, goat hair, and ash, could stand up to 18 meters high and often had a subterranean storage space. The design facilitated the cooling process by channeling breezes to the base and promoting the heat's rise out the top, effectively lowering the inside temperature to below freezing at night. This allowed not only for the making and storage of ice collected during winter but also for preserving food in the hot climate, demonstrating an early form of natural refrigeration.

The Byzantine Flame Thrower: Early Incendiary Weapons

The Byzantine Empire was renowned for its military innovations, including the development of the early flame thrower, known as "Greek fire." Used primarily at sea from the 7th century onward, Greek fire was a fiercely burning liquid composed of secret ingredients, believed to include naphtha and quicklime. When sprayed onto enemy ships using pressurized siphons, it could continue burning while floating on water. This formidable weapon was crucial in naval battles, particularly during sieges when ships were a significant threat. The exact composition of Greek fire was a closely guarded state secret, giving the Byzantines a significant advantage against their enemies and earning a fearsome reputation across the medieval world.

The Harappan Sewer System: Indus Valley Hygiene

The Harappan civilization, flourishing around 2600-1900 BCE in the Indus Valley, is credited with one of the world's earliest sophisticated urban sanitation systems. Each house in major cities like Mohenjo-Daro and Harappa had access to water and was connected to an extensive covered drainage system. These drains lined the major streets and were built with precise brickwork and gentle slopes to ensure the efficient removal of waste and stormwater. Remarkably, this advanced sewer system emphasizes the Harappans' prioritization of cleanliness and public health, underlining their advanced urban planning and engineering skills which were unparalleled in the contemporary world.

John Logie Baird's Pioneering Television Demonstration

In 1926, John Logie Baird demonstrated the first working television, showcasing the potential for transmitting moving images. His mechanical television system used spinning disks to create and display images, marking a significant milestone in the development of broadcast technology. Although vastly different from today's electronic televisions, Baird's invention laid the foundation for the television industry, revolutionizing the way people access and consume visual media.

Chapter Five
Culinary Conundrums

The Black Chicken: A Rare Breed with Dark Mystique

The Ayam Cemani, a rare breed of chicken from Indonesia, is known for its striking all-black appearance, which extends beyond its feathers to include its skin, muscles, organs, and even its bones. The breed's unique coloration is the result of a genetic condition known as fibromelanosis, which causes excessive pigmentation. While strikingly unusual, this characteristic does not affect the taste of the meat or eggs, though both are considered a delicacy in many parts of Southeast Asia. The Ayam Cemani is often associated with local folklore and is believed to possess mystical powers, making it a sought-after breed for both practical and ceremonial purposes.

Casu Marzu: The Forbidden Cheese

Casu Marzu is a traditional Sardinian cheese that has gained notoriety due to its unusual production process, which involves the deliberate introduction of live insect larvae. Derived from Pecorino, Casu Marzu goes beyond typical fermentation to a stage of decomposition, brought about by the digestive action of the larvae of the cheese fly, *Piophila casei*. These larvae are introduced to the cheese, and their digestion of the cheese fats helps to produce a very soft, creamy texture and a strong flavor that is highly prized by aficionados. Due to health concerns associated with consuming live larvae, which can survive in the intestine, Casu Marzu has been banned in the EU, but it remains available on the black market and is cherished by local Sardinians for its cultural and gastronomic significance.

The Lost Recipe of Garum: Ancient Rome's Favorite Condiment

Garum was a staple condiment in ancient Rome, made from fermenting fish, particularly intestines, in salt brine to create a potent, salty fish sauce. Highly prized across the Roman Empire for its ability to enhance flavors and for its supposed medicinal qualities, garum was used much like modern soy sauce or fish sauces in Southeast Asian cuisine. Despite its popularity in ancient times, the precise recipes and techniques used to make garum were largely lost with the decline of the Roman Empire. Today, culinary historians and chefs are experimenting with historical texts to recreate this flavorful sauce, aiming to bring a taste of ancient Roman culinary life to the modern palate.

Hákarl: The Fermented Shark of Iceland

Hákarl is a traditional Icelandic dish made from Greenland shark, a species that is naturally toxic due to high levels of urea and trimethylamine oxide in its flesh. To make hákarl edible, the shark is first buried in a shallow pit and pressed with stones to expel fluids, then left to ferment for 6-12 weeks. After this, the shark is cut into strips and hung to dry for several months. The result is a strong-smelling and distinctively flavored dish that is considered a delicacy in Iceland. This unique fermentation process not only neutralizes the toxins but also contributes to hákarl's pungent aroma and taste, which many describe as an acquired taste.

Century Eggs: A Timeless Chinese Delicacy

Century eggs, also known as thousand-year eggs, pidan, or preserved eggs, are a traditional Chinese delicacy made by preserving duck, chicken, or quail eggs in a mixture of clay, ash, salt, quicklime, and rice hulls for several weeks to several months. Despite their name, century eggs do not actually age for a century; the preservation process typically lasts just a few weeks to a few months. During this time, the yolk becomes dark green or gray with a creamy consistency, while the egg white turns into a dark brown, translucent jelly with a salty flavor. The transformation occurs through a series of chemical reactions that enhance the egg's flavor, making it a prized ingredient in many Chinese dishes.

The Mystery of the Last Supper's Menu

The Last Supper, famously depicted by Leonardo da Vinci, has intrigued scholars not only for its artistic value but also for the mystery surrounding the menu at this pivotal event. While traditional accounts based on the Gospels suggest that Jesus and his disciples likely consumed bread and wine, historical and cultural analyses propose that the meal might have also included other foods typical of a Jewish Passover meal at the time, such as lamb, bitter herbs, and unleavened bread. Some researchers even suggest the presence of foods like olives, dates, and fish, based on common dietary practices in ancient Jerusalem. This blend of historical and religious speculation continues to add layers of fascination to one of the most famous meals in human history.

Surströmming: Sweden's Pungent Fish Specialty

Surströmming, a traditional Swedish delicacy, is notorious for its strong odor and distinctive taste. This fermented Baltic Sea herring has been a part of Swedish cuisine since at least the 16th century. The fish is caught just prior to spawning in spring and then fermented in barrels for a couple of months before being tinned, where the fermentation continues for at least another six months. Upon opening, the cans often release a powerful burst of odor due to the ongoing fermentation. Despite its pungent smell, which many compare to rotten eggs, surströmming is cherished in Sweden, typically served with flatbreads, boiled potatoes, and fresh onions, and is celebrated with tasting parties during the late summer.

The Enigmatic Origins of Ketchup

Ketchup, a staple condiment in many modern diets, has surprisingly ancient and international origins that do not begin with tomatoes. Its precursor was a fermented fish sauce known as "ke-tsiap" originating from southeastern China in the 17th century. This sauce was made from pickled fish and spices, serving as a base for a variety of condiments across Asia. British explorers encountered it in the 18th century, brought it back to Europe, and began adapting it with ingredients like mushrooms and walnuts. It wasn't until the 19th century in America that tomatoes were added, transforming it into the sweet and tangy tomato ketchup widely consumed today. This evolution from a savory fish brine to a sweet tomato sauce illustrates the complex journey of global cuisine through trade and cultural exchange.

Fugu: The Deadly Delicacy

Fugu, or pufferfish, is a Japanese delicacy famous for its potential lethality. The fish contains tetrodotoxin, a potent neurotoxin that can be fatal if consumed in even small amounts. Chefs must undergo rigorous training for several years and obtain a special license to prepare and serve fugu safely. The allure of fugu lies not just in its flavor, which is subtle and delicate, but also in the thrill and prestige associated with eating a dish that has been prepared with such high stakes. Despite its dangers, fugu remains a sought-after dish, exemplifying the intricate balance between risk and culinary craftsmanship in Japanese cuisine.

The Unidentified Meat of Medieval Cockentrice

The medieval dish known as cockentrice was a culinary spectacle that combined different meats in a fantastical way, embodying the creativity of banquet chefs during the Middle Ages. This dish involved sewing the upper body of a suckling pig to the lower half of a capon or turkey, creating an exotic, hybrid creature that was then roasted. The cockentrice not only showcased the artistry and humor of medieval cooks but also highlighted their skill in crafting dishes that could delight and surprise guests at grand feasts. This type of culinary invention added an element of theatricality to dining, making meals a form of entertainment as well as nourishment.

The Elusive Recipe of Coca-Cola

The recipe for Coca-Cola is one of the most closely guarded secrets in the business world, stored in a high-security vault within the World of Coca-Cola museum in Atlanta, Georgia. Created in 1886 by pharmacist John S. Pemberton, the original formula called "Merchandise 7X" has been shrouded in secrecy to protect its unique flavor and brand. Only a very few executives know the complete recipe at any given time, and it's said that they are not allowed to travel together to ensure the safety of the secret. This intense confidentiality has not only fueled curiosity and lore surrounding the drink but has also been a key marketing feature, adding to Coca-Cola's mystique and global success.

Lutefisk: The Lye-Soaked Fish of Scandinavia

Lutefisk is a traditional Scandinavian dish made from dried whitefish, usually cod, which is soaked in cold water for several days, then in a lye solution for another period, before being soaked in fresh water again to make it edible. The lye treatment causes the fish to swell and become gelatinous. Historically, this method was used to preserve fish for storage and transport before the advent of refrigeration. Today, lutefisk is commonly served during the winter holidays, particularly in Norway and among Scandinavian communities in the United States, often accompanied by boiled potatoes, mushy peas, and bacon. Despite its strong, somewhat acquired taste and peculiar texture, lutefisk remains a cherished link to Nordic heritage.

The Disputed Origins of the Pavlova

The origin of the pavlova, a meringue-based dessert named after the Russian ballerina Anna Pavlova, is a subject of friendly dispute between Australia and New Zealand. Both countries claim to have invented it in the 1920s when Pavlova visited during her tour of the region. The dessert is known for its crisp crust and soft, light inside, usually topped with fruit and whipped cream. Despite extensive research into the dessert's origins, culinary historians have not conclusively determined its true birthplace, although New Zealand's claim is often supported by more documented recipes from earlier dates. Regardless of its origins, the pavlova remains a beloved treat in both countries, often featured during celebrations and festive seasons.

Ambergris: From Whale Vomit to Culinary Gold

Ambergris, often referred to as "whale vomit," is a highly valued substance in the perfume industry, known for its ability to fix scent to human skin. It originates as a bile duct secretion of sperm whales, which can help the animals facilitate the digestion of sharp objects like squid beaks. It is rare; not all sperm whales produce it, and it must float in the ocean for years, during which it hardens and develops a sweet, earthy scent before being found. Historically, ambergris was also used in cooking, especially in the Middle Ages, as an ingredient in luxurious dishes for its flavor-enhancing properties. Today, it continues to be a coveted ingredient in high-end perfumes, fetching prices that can exceed the value of gold by weight.

The Vanishing Art of Saffron Farming

Saffron farming, known for producing one of the world's most expensive spices, involves a labor-intensive process that contributes to its high cost. Derived from the crocus flower, specifically Crocus sativus, each flower produces only three stigmas, which are hand-picked during a very short annual blooming season. It takes about 75,000 saffron crocus flowers to produce a single pound of saffron spice. The meticulous cultivation and harvest processes, combined with the large quantity of flowers needed, make saffron farming a vanishing art, as the economic feasibility dwindles and fewer farmers undertake its production. Despite these challenges, saffron remains highly prized for its unique flavor, color, and medicinal properties, celebrated in culinary and cultural practices around the globe.

The Mysterious Meat of the Dodo Bird

The dodo bird, a flightless bird native to Mauritius, became extinct in the late 17th century, and surprisingly little is known about its taste and culinary use. Early accounts from Dutch sailors, who were among the few to consume the bird, suggest that its meat was not particularly esteemed; some described it as tough and unpalatable. The dodo's size, similar to that of a turkey, would have provided a considerable amount of meat, but its reputation among sailors and settlers for its flavor was mixed at best. Today, the dodo is often cited as an example of human-driven extinction, and its meat remains a mystery, wrapped in the enigma of a bird that vanished before modern scientific study could document it comprehensively.

The Ghost Chili Pepper: A Spicy Enigma

The Ghost Chili Pepper, also known as Bhut Jolokia, is renowned for being one of the hottest chili peppers in the world. Originating in the northeastern region of India, this pepper was once confirmed by Guinness World Records as the hottest chili pepper on the planet. The Ghost Chili achieves its intense heat through a high concentration of capsaicin, which can exceed 1 million Scoville heat units. This level of spiciness not only makes it a challenge even for daring spice enthusiasts but also has practical applications in Indian folk medicine and as an elephant deterrent by incorporating it into smoke bombs. Its cultivation and use reflect deep cultural traditions as well as modern culinary adventurism.

The Unexplained Absence of the Tomato in Italian Cuisine Until the 16th Century

Tomatoes, now a cornerstone of Italian cuisine, were absent from Italy until the 16th century because they are native to the Americas. Following the Spanish colonization of the Americas, tomatoes were brought to Europe, where they were initially met with suspicion and were grown as ornamental plants due to fears they were poisonous. It wasn't until the late 17th or early 18th century that tomatoes were widely adopted into Italian cooking, revolutionizing the cuisine with dishes like marinara sauce and Margherita pizza. The delay in their culinary use highlights the initial cultural and gastronomic hesitations that often accompany the introduction of new food items across different societies.

The Cryptic Culinary Use of Dragon's Blood

Dragon's blood, a bright red resin obtained from different species of a number of distinct plant genera like *Dracaena, Daemonorops,* and *Croton,* has a name that evokes mythical imagery, though its uses are grounded in reality. Historically, this resin has not only been used for its medicinal and dye properties but also in incense and varnish. Interestingly, it has also been used in culinary contexts, particularly as a coloring agent in alcoholic beverages to impart a vibrant red hue. The intriguing name and vivid color of dragon's blood make it a subject of curiosity and a unique ingredient in both traditional remedies and culinary experiments.

The Controversial History of Foie Gras

Foie gras, a luxury food product made from the liver of ducks or geese that have been specially fattened, has a controversial history rooted in its production method. Dating back to ancient Egypt, where humans first observed the natural fattening of wild geese, the practice was later adopted and refined in Roman and medieval French cuisines. Today, foie gras is praised for its rich, buttery flavor and smooth texture, but it faces significant ethical debates due to the force-feeding process known as "gavage." This method, necessary for enlarging the birds' livers, has led to legal bans and restrictions in several countries, making foie gras a focal point in discussions about animal welfare and culinary tradition.

The Unusual Ingredient of Bird's Nest Soup

Bird's Nest Soup, a prized delicacy in Chinese cuisine, is made from the nests of the edible-nest swiftlet, birds that use their saliva to construct their nests. The nests, once harvested, are valued for their unique gelatinous texture when dissolved in water and are believed to offer various health benefits, including enhancing skin elasticity and boosting the immune system. These nests are among the most expensive animal products consumed by humans, with prices soaring due to high demand and the labor-intensive process of collecting them from cave walls or house eaves, where the swiftlets reside. The rarity and supposed health benefits make Bird's Nest Soup a sought-after luxury in many parts of Asia.

The Lost Flavor of Silphium

Silphium, a plant once highly prized in ancient Mediterranean civilizations, is believed to have gone extinct by the first century AD, largely due to overharvesting. Native to the region of Cyrenaica (modern-day Libya), silphium was renowned for its diverse uses, notably in cooking, medicine, and even as a purported contraceptive. The plant's exact flavor and properties remain a mystery today, as its true identity has been lost to history, with some speculating it was related to the fennel family. The high demand for silphium, its depicted use on Cyrenian coins, and references by ancient authors like Pliny the Elder underscore its cultural and economic importance. The loss of silphium is a classic example of the ecological impacts of human exploitation.

The Conflicting Accounts of the First Thanksgiving Menu

The traditional narrative of the first Thanksgiving in 1621, celebrated by the Plymouth colonists and Wampanoag Native Americans, often features turkey as the centerpiece. However, historical accounts suggest a more diverse menu. According to primary sources, including a letter from colonist Edward Winslow, the feast likely included venison, brought by the Wampanoag guests, and various types of fowl, which could have included ducks, geese, or turkeys. Additionally, seafood such as fish, clams, and mussels were abundant in the region and may have been part of the meal. The inclusion of native fruits, vegetables, and grains like corn further reflects the blend of European agricultural practices and Native American food traditions that characterized the early years of colonial interaction.

The Secret Spice Blends of Medieval Europe

Medieval Europe's cuisine was distinctly characterized by its liberal use of various spices, a practice partly driven by the desire to mask the taste of preserved, less-fresh meats. Spices such as black pepper, cinnamon, cloves, nutmeg, and saffron were highly prized and often reflected one's social status due to their expense and rarity. These spices were typically imported from Asia and the Middle East through complex trade routes, making them a luxury. Notably, the precise combinations of these spices were closely guarded secrets among cooks, who developed specific blends to create unique and sought-after flavors. These spice blends not only added depth to European dishes but also served as early forms of culinary expression and identity.

The Inexplicable Popularity of the Twinkie

The Twinkie, an iconic American snack cake, first introduced by Hostess Brands in 1930, has garnered an inexplicable popularity that has endured for decades. Originally filled with banana cream, its filling was switched to vanilla after a banana shortage during World War II. One of the most enduring myths about Twinkies is their shelf life, often joked to be virtually eternal due to preservatives. In reality, the Twinkie's shelf life is approximately 45 days, much shorter than the legend suggests. The Twinkie has become a cultural icon, celebrated in films, literature, and even courtrooms, where the "Twinkie Defense" highlighted its unexpected role in American legal history.

The Elusive True Flavor of Vanilla

Vanilla, one of the world's most popular and expensive spices after saffron, is derived from the orchids of the genus *Vanilla*. Originally cultivated by the Totonac people of Mexico, vanilla's true flavor is far more complex than many of the synthetic vanilla extracts commonly used today. Real vanilla flavor comes from the compound vanillin, along with several hundred other compounds present in the beans. The process of curing vanilla beans involves sun-drying and sweating the beans over several months, which develops its rich, deep flavor. The complexity and labor-intensiveness of this process contribute to natural vanilla's rich taste and high cost, making genuine vanilla a culinary treasure.

The Mysterious Origins of Worcestershire Sauce

Worcestershire sauce, a staple in kitchens worldwide, has a mysterious and accidental origin story that dates back to the 1830s in Worcester, England. The sauce was developed by two chemists, John Wheeley Lea and William Perrins, who were attempting to replicate a recipe brought back from India by Lord Sandys, a nobleman of the area. After mixing the ingredients, they found the initial result unpalatable and stored it in barrels in their cellar. Upon rediscovering the barrels a few years later, they tasted the fermented mixture again and found that it had transformed into a deliciously complex sauce. They began bottling and selling it as Lea & Perrins Worcestershire Sauce, and it quickly became a culinary sensation, renowned for its unique blend of tangy, savory, and sweet flavors.

The Enigmatic Edibility of the Platypus

The platypus, one of Australia's most unusual and iconic mammals, poses a peculiar puzzle regarding its edibility. This semi-aquatic creature, known for its duck-like bill, beaver-like tail, and otter-like feet, is also one of the few mammals that produce venom. Male platypuses have spurs on their hind limbs that can deliver a venom capable of causing severe pain to humans, thus complicating any thoughts of the platypus as a food source. Moreover, the platypus is protected under Australian law, making it illegal to capture or harm them, further cementing its status more as a subject of scientific fascination than as a culinary delicacy.

The Disputed Roots of the Potato Chip

The potato chip, a ubiquitous snack enjoyed worldwide, has its origins steeped in culinary legend. According to popular lore, potato chips were accidentally invented in 1853 by George Crum, a chef at the Moon Lake Lodge resort in Saratoga Springs, New York. The story goes that a dissatisfied customer repeatedly sent his French-fried potatoes back to the kitchen, complaining that they were too thick and soggy. In a fit of pique, Crum sliced the potatoes as thinly as possible, fried them until crisp, and salted them heavily. To his surprise, the customer loved them, and the "Saratoga Chips" quickly became a favorite. While this story is widely recounted, researchers have found references to similar recipes in earlier cookbooks, suggesting that the concept of frying thin potato slices may have existed before Crum's supposed invention. Nonetheless, Crum's iteration captured the public's imagination and set the standard for what would become one of the world's favorite snacks.

The Uncertain Culinary Use of the Oracle Bone

Oracle bones, primarily used during the Shang dynasty in ancient China for divination purposes, also hold a lesser-known connection to culinary history. These bones, which were mostly turtle plastrons and ox scapulae, were inscribed with questions concerning future events, from weather to warfare, and then subjected to heat until they cracked; the patterns of the cracks were interpreted by diviners to predict outcomes. While their use in cooking is not directly documented, the preparation process involved intense heating, akin to roasting, which suggests that these practices could intersect with food preparation techniques of the time. Moreover, the ritual importance of food offerings in divination rituals, where bones might have been used both as tools and as part of ceremonial meals, highlights a complex relationship between culinary and religious practices in ancient China.

The Puzzling Flavor Profile of Durian

Durian, often referred to as the "king of fruits" in Southeast Asia, is notorious for its divisive flavor profile and overpowering aroma, which has been variously compared to rotten onions, turpentine, and raw sewage. This tropical fruit's creamy texture and complex flavor are beloved by many, yet repulsive to others. The unique combination of esters, ketones, and aldehydes in durian creates a multifaceted flavor that includes sweet, almond-like tones underneath the pungent odor. This intriguing complexity makes durian a subject of fascination and cultural pride in its native regions, while its strong aroma has led to its ban in many public spaces, such as hotels and public transport systems across Southeast Asia.

The Unexplained Decline of the Roman Condiment Defrutum

Defrutum was a popular condiment in ancient Rome, made by reducing fresh grape must to create a thick, sweet syrup. This versatile ingredient was used extensively in Roman cooking to sweeten dishes, add flavor to sauces, and even as a preservative for fruits and other foods. Despite its widespread use in the Roman culinary world, defrutum's popularity declined sharply as the Roman Empire fell, largely due to the disruption of traditional vineyard cultivation and changes in trade routes, which affected the availability of key ingredients. Additionally, evolving culinary tastes and the adoption of new flavoring substances like sugar, introduced through expanding trade with the East, contributed to the disappearance of defrutum from the culinary repertoire, leaving it as little more than a footnote in culinary history.

The Ambiguous Ingredients of Medieval Cocktails

Medieval cocktails, often concocted in monasteries and courts across Europe, were composed of a mix of ingredients that may seem unusual today. These early alcoholic beverages, known as "piment" or "hypocras," typically blended wine or ale with a variety of spices like cinnamon, ginger, and nutmeg, as well as honey for sweetness. Interestingly, some recipes also included ingredients like ambergris and musk, which are more commonly associated with perfumery than with cooking. This eclectic use of ingredients reflected the medieval palate's preference for complex flavors and also the period's limited understanding of distillation techniques, leading to creative combinations to enhance the flavors and purported medicinal benefits of these drinks.

The Enigmatic Appeal of Licorice

Licorice, derived from the root of the plant *Glycyrrhiza glabra*, has been used for thousands of years not only as a candy flavoring but also for its medicinal properties. The distinctive taste of licorice comes from the compound glycyrrhizin, which is up to 50 times sweeter than sugar. This plant has been historically valued across many cultures, from ancient Egypt, where it was found in great quantities in King Tutankhamun's tomb, to modern times as a staple in traditional Chinese medicine. The enduring appeal of licorice is somewhat enigmatic, given its polarizing taste, while some people cherish its complex, sweet, and slightly bitter flavor, others find it distinctly unpalatable.

The Unknown Taste of the Mammoth

The woolly mammoth, a close relative of today's elephants, roamed the Earth thousands of years ago before becoming extinct. Despite its disappearance, there have been rare instances where well-preserved mammoth meat has been discovered in the frozen tundras of Siberia and Alaska. On a few occasions, adventurous scientists and indigenous peoples have tasted mammoth meat, though reports on its flavor vary significantly. Some claim it tastes extremely unpalatable due to its state of decay and freeze-burning, while others describe it as something akin to extremely gamey, oily meat. The idea of tasting a species that walked the Earth over 4,000 years ago adds a layer of intrigue and mystery to the mammoth's profile in both scientific and culinary contexts.

The Secret Formula of Chartreuse

Chartreuse is a French liqueur made by Carthusian Monks since the 1740s according to a secret recipe said to contain 130 herbs, plants, and flowers. The recipe is known only to two monks at any given time, ensuring a high level of secrecy. This mysterious concoction originated from an ancient manuscript given to the monks in 1605 and has never been fully decoded by outsiders. The liqueur is renowned not only for its unique and complex flavor profile but also for its distinct vibrant green and yellow colors, naturally derived from the botanicals used. Chartreuse remains a popular ingredient in cocktails and is prized for its rich history and artisanal production method.

The Mysterious Disappearance of the Szechuan Peppercorn

The Szechuan peppercorn, famous for its unique numbing sensation and a staple in Chinese cuisine, faced a mysterious disappearance from U.S. markets when it was banned by the USDA in 1968. The ban was due to concerns that the peppercorns could carry a bacterial disease capable of threatening the American citrus crop. For decades, this left American chefs and food enthusiasts without a legal means to access this essential ingredient of Szechuan cuisine. It wasn't until 2005 that the ban was lifted, under the condition that the peppercorns be heat-treated to kill any potentially harmful bacteria. The return of Szechuan peppercorn revitalized authentic Szechuan cooking in the U.S., reintroducing its thrilling tingling effect to dishes.

The Unclear Origins of the Hot Dog

The hot dog, a staple of American cuisine, actually traces its roots to Europe, but its exact origin remains somewhat unclear. Most food historians agree that the modern hot dog evolved from sausages developed in Germany, particularly in Frankfurt and Vienna, which gave rise to terms like "frankfurter" and "wiener." These sausages were brought to the United States by German immigrants in the 19th century. The practice of serving these sausages in buns, which led to the birth of the hot dog as we know it today, is believed to have started to make them easier to eat on the go at fairs, carnivals, and ball games. This convenient adaptation quickly caught on, embedding the hot dog into the fabric of American fast food culture.

The Lost Art of Roman Fish Sauce

Roman fish sauce, known as garum, was a culinary staple in ancient Rome, highly valued for its ability to enhance flavors much like modern soy sauce. Made from fermenting fish, especially small ones, with salt, the sauce was produced in large quantities and exported extensively throughout the Roman Empire. Garum was so integral to Roman cooking that it was produced using a variety of recipes, often graded by quality and price. Despite its popularity in antiquity, the traditional method of making garum was eventually lost after the fall of the Roman Empire. Interest in this ancient condiment has been revived recently, with historians and chefs exploring historical texts to recreate the legendary sauce.

The Peculiar Taste of Miracle Fruit

Miracle fruit, or *Synsepalum dulcificum*, is a remarkable berry native to West Africa that possesses the unique ability to modify taste perceptions. The fruit contains a glycoprotein called miraculin, which binds to taste bud receptors and temporarily makes sour foods taste sweet. After consuming miracle fruit, the flavor of a lemon can resemble that of lemonade without any added sugar, and strawberries can taste candied. This unusual property has made miracle fruit a subject of interest for dietary experimentation, potentially aiding those looking to reduce sugar intake. Its effects last up to an hour, offering a truly unique gustatory experience that turns any sour taste delightfully sweet.

The Enigmatic Flavor of Mountain Dew

Mountain Dew, the popular citrus-flavored soda, has a unique and somewhat enigmatic taste that has been difficult to categorically define since its creation in the 1940s. Originally developed as a mixer for whiskey, its flavor profile is distinctively zesty and sweet but does not distinctly resemble any specific type of citrus fruit. Over the years, Mountain Dew has become known for its high caffeine content compared to other sodas and its vibrant neon color. Its original formula has also been adapted into a wide array of flavors and variations, yet the classic version remains a favorite, particularly among gamers and extreme sports enthusiasts for its energizing effects and bold taste.

The Mystery Meat of Spam

Spam, the canned meat product made primarily from pork, was first introduced by Hormel Foods Corporation in 1937 and gained iconic status during World War II. It was shipped overseas in vast quantities to feed Allied troops, providing a high-protein food source that required no refrigeration. The ingredients list of Spam is surprisingly simple, typically consisting of pork with ham meat added, salt, water, modified potato starch as a binder, sugar, and sodium nitrite as a preservative. Despite its straightforward composition, Spam has inspired a range of culinary uses across the globe, from sushi rolls in Japan to fried rice in Hawaii, making it a versatile and enduringly popular item in international cuisine. Its exact flavor profile, often described as salty and meaty with a slightly spiced and processed taste, remains a unique culinary enigma cherished by many.

The Obscure Recipe of Ancient Egyptian Bread

Ancient Egyptian bread was a staple in the diet of the pharaohs and the populace alike, and its preparation involved unique methods and ingredients that have intrigued historians. Made primarily from emmer wheat or barley, the bread often contained grit and sand from the milling process, which would wear down teeth, evident in dental analyses of mummified remains. Yeast was not a known ingredient then; instead, the Egyptians likely utilized natural yeast present in the environment to ferment the dough. Interestingly, they also shaped their bread into various forms, some resembling animals and others symbolic shapes, which were not only consumed daily but also placed in tombs as offerings for the afterlife. The methods and recipes, though not fully clear today, highlight the Egyptians' advanced baking skills and the cultural significance of bread in their society.

The Enigmatic Edibility of the Acorn

Acorns were a vital food source for many ancient civilizations and continue to be consumed in various parts of the world. Rich in nutrients, acorns require extensive processing to remove tannins, which are bitter compounds that can be toxic in high quantities. Indigenous peoples, particularly in North America, developed sophisticated methods to leach these tannins, often by grinding the acorns into a meal and washing it in a stream or boiling it. The resulting acorn flour is versatile, used to make bread, cakes, and even as a thickening agent in stews. Today, acorns are re-emerging as a sustainable, gluten-free food option, reflecting a growing interest in traditional and foraged foods.

The Mysterious Origins of Mustard

Mustard, one of the world's oldest condiments, traces its origins back over thousands of years. Archaeologists have discovered traces of mustard seeds in prehistoric settlements dating back to 2300 BC. Ancient civilizations, including the Sumerians, Romans, and Greeks, utilized mustard seeds not only for their culinary flavor but also for their medicinal properties. The Romans were likely the first to experiment with making a paste from mustard seeds, which they mixed with grape juice, known as "must," leading to the name "mustard." This practice was refined over centuries, spreading across Europe and evolving into the varieties of mustard we know today, from the classic French Dijon to the robust English mustards.

The Unexplained Popularity of Bubble Tea

Bubble tea, originating from Taiwan in the 1980s, has gained international popularity, characterized by its signature tapioca pearls and a wide array of flavors. This drink was initially created as a unique twist on traditional tea by combining it with milk and the chewy pearls, adding not just flavor but also an engaging texture. The "bubbles" in bubble tea can refer both to the tapioca pearls at the bottom and the frothy foam created when the tea is shaken before serving. The versatile nature of bubble tea, allowing for countless combinations of tea bases, toppings like jellies and popping boba, and sweetness levels, caters to a broad range of tastes and personal preferences, fueling its global spread and enduring appeal.

The Lost Technique of Medieval Meat Smoking

Medieval meat smoking was an essential technique used across Europe, not only to flavor meats but to preserve them in the days before refrigeration. This process involved exposing meat to smoke from burning or smoldering material, usually wood, which helped to extend the shelf life of the food by impeding the growth of bacteria. Different woods imparted different flavors, and the technique varied from region to region. Interestingly, many of the specific recipes and wood types used in medieval smoking have been lost to time, as the oral tradition that carried these methods was not always documented. This has left historians and culinary experts piecing together clues from archaeological findings and ancient texts to rediscover the flavors of the past.

Why Pineapples Tenderize Meat

Pineapples contain a unique enzyme called bromelain, which has the remarkable ability to break down proteins. This makes pineapple an excellent natural meat tenderizer. When pineapple or its juice is used in marinades, the bromelain efficiently softens meat by cleaving the peptide bonds in the proteins, making the texture more tender. This enzymatic activity is so potent that if left marinating too long, the meat can become too soft or mushy. Cooking neutralizes bromelain's tenderizing effect, which is why pineapple must be fresh if used for tenderizing purposes. This natural tenderizing property has been utilized in various cuisines around the world to enhance the texture and flavor of meats.

The Puzzle of Pre-Columbian Popcorn

Popcorn is not a modern snack but rather has ancient roots, especially in the Americas where it has been a staple for millennia. Archaeological evidence in Peru suggests that popcorn was consumed by Pre-Columbian peoples as early as 4700 BC, making it one of the oldest forms of corn consumption. The kernels found in these ancient sites were from a variety of corn that pops when heated, indicating that these early civilizations recognized and utilized the specific properties of popcorn. This ancient snack was not only eaten but also used for decoration on clothing and other ceremonial purposes, highlighting its cultural significance. The tradition of popping corn was so prevalent that it continued largely unchanged into modern times, transcending centuries to remain a popular snack.

The Unresolved Debate Over the Origin of Tea

Tea, one of the world's oldest and most beloved beverages, has an origin steeped in legend and conflicting historical accounts. While China is traditionally credited with the discovery of tea, with mythical Emperor Shennong purportedly encountering it in 2737 BC when leaves drifted into his boiling water, other regions also claim early tea usage. For instance, records suggest that tea plants were native and used in parts of India and what is now Myanmar long before Chinese influence. This has led to a fascinating debate among historians and botanists regarding where tea was first used and cultivated, highlighting its importance in ancient cultures and its global journey to becoming a staple in diets around the world.

Chapter Six

Natural Wonders of the World

Tsingy de Bemaraha: Madagascar's Limestone Forest

Tsingy de Bemaraha National Park in Madagascar is renowned for its dramatic landscape of sharp limestone pinnacles known as "tsingy," which means "where one cannot walk barefoot" in the Malagasy language. This UNESCO World Heritage site spans over 666 square kilometers and features a unique geological formation created by the erosion of limestone rocks, resulting in a jagged forest of needle-like towers that can reach several meters in height. The park is not only a spectacle of natural beauty but also a biodiversity hotspot, home to various endemic species of plants and animals that have adapted to its extreme and isolated environment, including several types of lemurs that navigate this perilous terrain.

The Fairy Pools: Natural Beauty in Scotland's Isle of Skye

The Fairy Pools, located on the Isle of Skye in Scotland, are a mesmerizing series of clear, cold pools and waterfalls formed by streams flowing down from the Cuillin Mountains. These vibrant, azure pools are renowned for their almost supernatural clarity and color, which are so vivid they seem otherworldly. The pools attract adventurers and photographers from around the world, drawn not only by their natural beauty but also by the challenge of the icy water, which is popular for wild swimming. The enchanting setting of the Fairy Pools, complete with natural arches and picturesque landscapes, contributes to their mystique and the local legends of fairies, enhancing Skye's reputation as a place of magical, untouched wilderness.

The Great Barrier Reef: Underwater Paradise

The Great Barrier Reef, located off the coast of Queensland, Australia, is the world's largest coral reef system and one of the most biodiverse areas on the planet. Spanning over 2,300 kilometers, it is composed of over 2,900 individual reefs and 900 islands. This reef system is so vast that it is the only living structure on Earth visible from space. The Great Barrier Reef is home to thousands of species of marine life, including over 1,500 species of fish, 400 species of coral, and a wide range of sharks, mollusks, and birds. It not only serves as a critical habitat for these species but also plays a significant role in global environmental health, such as carbon and nitrogen fixing, which benefits the entire planet.

Victoria Falls: The Smoke That Thunders

Victoria Falls, known locally as Mosi-oa-Tunya, meaning "The Smoke That Thunders," is one of the largest and most famous waterfalls in the world. Located on the Zambezi River at the border between Zambia and Zimbabwe, this natural wonder stands at about 108 meters high and 1,708 meters wide. The immense force of the water plunging into the gorge below creates a mist that can rise up to 400 meters into the air and be visible from up to 50 kilometers away. This misty spray gives the falls its local name and supports a unique rainforest ecosystem adjacent to the waterfall. The spectacular sight attracts tourists from around the globe and is considered a major landmark of the African continent.

The Door to Hell: A Burning Natural Gas Field

The "Door to Hell" is a natural gas field in Derweze, Turkmenistan, that has been burning continuously since 1971. Originally a natural gas field being explored by Soviet scientists, the ground beneath the drilling rig collapsed, leaving a large hole with a diameter of about 70 meters. To prevent the dangerous release of methane gas, scientists decided to ignite it, hoping the fire would consume the gas within a few weeks. However, the gas continued to burn, and the site has become a bizarre tourist attraction, known for its eerie and mesmerizing glow visible from a distance, especially at night. The relentless flames create a dramatic visual, making it appear as a fiery gateway to the underworld.

Aurora Borealis: The Northern Lights

The Aurora Borealis, commonly known as the Northern Lights, is a natural light display predominantly seen in high-latitude regions around the Arctic. This stunning phenomenon occurs when charged particles from the sun collide with atoms in Earth's atmosphere, causing bursts of light that illuminate the sky in a spectrum of vibrant colors. The most common hue observed is a brilliant green, produced by oxygen molecules located about 60 miles above the earth, though pinks, violets, yellows, and blues can also appear depending on the altitude and type of gas involved. The lights are best viewed in a belt known as the "auroral zone," which is typically 3 to 6 degrees wide in latitude and between 10 and 20 degrees from the geomagnetic poles, making locations like Norway, Sweden, and Canada prime viewing spots.

The Dead Sea: A Saltwater Lake

The Dead Sea, located at the lowest point on Earth's surface, is a salt lake bordered by Jordan to the east and Israel and the West Bank to the west. Its shores are about 430 meters below sea level, making it the Earth's lowest elevation on land. The lake is renowned for its exceptionally high salt concentration, which averages around 34%—nearly ten times saltier than the ocean. This extreme salinity prevents most aquatic life from thriving, hence the name "Dead Sea." The high density of the water makes swimming more like floating, offering a unique experience where it is almost impossible to sink. This unusual feature, combined with the mineral-rich mud, attracts tourists seeking therapeutic benefits and surreal water experiences.

Mount Kilimanjaro: Africa's Snow-Capped Giant

Mount Kilimanjaro, located in Tanzania, is the highest mountain in Africa, standing at about 5,895 meters (19,341 feet) above sea level. Remarkably, its summit, Uhuru Peak, is capped with snow and glaciers, despite being near the equator. This iconic snow cap is visible from miles away and dramatically contrasts with the surrounding savannah. Kilimanjaro is a stratovolcano that consists of three volcanic cones: Kibo, Mawenzi, and Shira. Of these, Kibo is the only dormant cone and could erupt again. The mountain's diverse ecosystems range from its base, covered with agricultural fields, through lush rainforest and alpine meadow zones, up to the barren, icy summit. The decreasing snow cap, attributed to global warming, has made Kilimanjaro a poignant symbol of environmental change.

Salar de Uyuni: The World's Largest Salt Flat

Salar de Uyuni in Bolivia is recognized as the world's largest salt flat, spanning an incredible 10,582 square kilometers (4,086 square miles). Formed from prehistoric lakes that evaporated long ago, the vast expanse is covered by a thick crust of salt, several meters deep in places, making it one of the most extraordinary landscapes on Earth. Underneath the crust are large reservoirs of lithium-rich brine, accounting for up to 70% of the world's lithium reserves, a vital component in battery production. During the rainy season, the flat is covered with a thin layer of water, transforming it into a stunning natural mirror that perfectly reflects the sky above, creating a surreal and captivating visual phenomenon that draws tourists and photographers from around the globe.

Niagara Falls: Power and Beauty

Niagara Falls, located on the border between Ontario, Canada, and New York, USA, is not only known for its breathtaking beauty but also for its substantial role in hydroelectric power production. Comprising three separate falls, Horseshoe Falls, American Falls, and Bridal Veil Falls, Niagara Falls has the highest flow rate of any waterfall in North America. Approximately 20% of the world's freshwater lies in the Great Lakes, and most of that flows over Niagara Falls. Since the late 19th century, the falls have been harnessed to generate power, making it one of the world's largest sources of hydroelectric power. The creation of this power has led to significant industrial growth in the region and helps power both New York State and Southern Ontario.

Antelope Canyon: A Sculpture Carved by Water

Antelope Canyon, located on Navajo land near Page, Arizona, is a stunning example of natural artistry, sculpted by the forces of water and wind over millions of years. This slot canyon is famous for its wave-like structure and the light beams that shine directly down into the openings of the canyon, creating breathtaking scenes. The narrow passageways between the smooth, undulating walls of sandstone appear to flow like water themselves, an effect heightened by the changing sunlight that filters down into the depths of the canyon. Formed primarily by flash flooding where the water, carrying sand, rushes through the rock, Antelope Canyon's corridors are a testament to the power of natural elements in shaping the Earth's surface, making it a photographer's and geologist's paradise.

The Sahara Desert: Vastness of Sand

The Sahara Desert, covering approximately 9 million square kilometers, is the largest hot desert in the world and the third largest desert overall, after Antarctica and the Arctic, which are cold deserts. Stretching across much of North Africa, the Sahara is as large as the continental United States, and is well-known for its harsh environment and extreme temperatures, which can fluctuate from one of the hottest places on earth by day to near freezing at night. Despite its arid reputation, the Sahara is not just endless sand dunes; it also comprises mountain ranges, rocky plateaus, and even seasonal lakes, supporting a surprisingly diverse range of life adapted to the harsh conditions. Historically, it was greener and more humid, with many rock paintings depicting wildlife and vegetation, providing evidence of a significantly wetter climate thousands of years ago.

Wulingyuan Scenic Area: A Forest of Quartzite Sandstone Pillars

Wulingyuan Scenic Area, located in the Hunan Province of China, is renowned for its spectacular landscape of over 3,000 quartzite sandstone pillars, some of which rise over 200 meters high. These striking formations are often shrouded in mist, creating a mystical atmosphere that has inspired many traditional Chinese paintings. The area's unique topography is the result of millions of years of physical erosion mainly due to expanding ice in winter and the lush vegetation cover that protects the base of the rocks but leaves the tops exposed to the elements. This geological wonder not only draws tourists and geologists alike but also served as the inspiration for the floating mountains in the blockbuster film "Avatar." Wulingyuan was designated a UNESCO World Heritage site in 1992 due to its outstanding natural beauty and its importance to the study of the history of Earth's climate and geological processes.

The Blue Hole: Belize's Submarine Sinkhole

The Great Blue Hole, located near the center of Lighthouse Reef off the coast of Belize, is a giant marine sinkhole that is circular in shape, measuring 318 meters across and 124 meters deep. Originally a limestone cave that formed during the last ice age, this structure collapsed and was submerged over 10,000 years ago as ocean levels rose. The Blue Hole is famed not only for its striking deep blue color, visible from the air, but also for its crystal-clear waters and diverse marine life, making it a hotspot for scuba divers around the world. Intriguingly, this underwater cavern holds massive stalactites and limestone formations, providing evidence of its geological history and attracting researchers and adventure divers alike to explore its depths.

Yellowstone National Park: Geothermal Wonders

Yellowstone National Park, established in 1872 as the world's first national park, is famed for its vast and diverse geothermal features, which include more than 10,000 hot springs, mudpots, fumaroles, and geysers. The park is situated atop a volcanic hot spot, which fuels its famous geothermal activity. One of the park's most iconic features, Old Faithful Geyser, is renowned for its predictable eruptions, occurring every 44 to 125 minutes, and is one of the most predictable geographical features on Earth. Yellowstone's unique landscape is not only a major draw for millions of tourists annually but also serves as an important natural laboratory for studying geothermal processes and ecosystem dynamics.

The Serengeti Plains: A Wildlife Spectacle

The Serengeti Plains in Tanzania are renowned worldwide for hosting the largest terrestrial mammal migration in the world. This vast ecosystem covers approximately 30,000 square kilometers and is home to over 2 million wildebeest, zebras, and gazelle that migrate in a seasonal pattern in search of water and fresh grazing. This migration is a staggering spectacle of nature, where herds traverse hundreds of kilometers in a predictable annual pattern, facing numerous predators such as lions, hyenas, and crocodiles along the way. The Serengeti's rich biodiversity and complex ecosystem have not only made it a focal point for conservation efforts but also a prime location for studying animal behavior and ecological processes, embodying the essence of the wild African landscape.

The Cliffs of Moher: Ireland's Majestic Coastline

The Cliffs of Moher, one of Ireland's most spectacular natural attractions, rise dramatically from the southwestern edge of the Burren region in County Clare. These cliffs soar 214 meters (702 feet) at their highest point above the Atlantic Ocean and stretch for about 14 kilometers (9 miles) along the coast. Formed over 320 million years ago during the Upper Carboniferous period, the cliffs consist primarily of shale and sandstone, with the oldest rocks visible at the bottom. They provide breathtaking views and are home to one of the major colonies of cliff-nesting seabirds in Ireland, including puffins, razorbills, and seagulls, making them not only a stunning geographical feature but also a vital habitat for diverse avian species.

Angel Falls: The World's Highest Waterfall

Angel Falls, located in Venezuela's Canaima National Park, holds the distinction of being the world's highest uninterrupted waterfall. The falls cascade from a height of 979 meters (3,212 feet), with water plunging over the edge of the Auyán-tepui mountain in the Guiana Highlands. Named after Jimmy Angel, an American aviator who first flew over the falls in 1933, this breathtaking natural wonder is roughly 15 times higher than Niagara Falls. Due to its remote location in the jungle, accessing the falls requires a river trip followed by a hike through dense rainforest, making a visit to Angel Falls a true adventure. The falls are also often shrouded in cloud mist, which can create spectacular rainbows, adding to their mystique and visual allure.

The Redwood Forests: Giants of California

The Redwood Forests of California are home to some of the oldest and tallest trees in the world, with many specimens towering over 300 feet. Among these, the coastal redwoods (Sequoia sempervirens) are the tallest living trees on Earth. These ancient giants can live for over 2,000 years and are found along the coastal region of Northern California, thriving in the moist, fog-laden air that is unique to this area. The forests not only provide a critical habitat for diverse ecosystems, including numerous endangered species, but also play a significant role in carbon storage, which is vital for climate regulation. Remarkably, the thick bark of redwoods makes them highly resistant to environmental disturbances such as fire and disease, contributing to their longevity and the stability of their ecosystems.

The Great Ocean Road: A Scenic Journey

The Great Ocean Road in Victoria, Australia, is not only famous for its breathtaking coastal scenery but also for its historical significance as the world's largest war memorial. Built by returned soldiers between 1919 and 1932 and dedicated to soldiers killed during World War I, the road stretches about 243 kilometers (151 miles) along the southeastern coast. This stunning route winds through varying terrain, offering views of rugged cliffs, serene beaches, and lush rainforests. It also passes by iconic landmarks such as the Twelve Apostles, limestone stacks that rise majestically from the Southern Ocean. The construction of the road was a monumental task intended to provide employment for returning soldiers while also creating a lasting tribute to those who died in the war, making it a poignant site of memory and beauty.

Mount Fuji: Japan's Iconic Peak

Mount Fuji, Japan's tallest and most iconic peak, stands at 3,776 meters (12,389 feet) and is an active stratovolcano that last erupted in 1707-1708. Located on Honshu Island, it is one of Japan's "Three Holy Mountains" and has been a pilgrimage site for centuries. Remarkably, Mount Fuji is actually a composite of three separate volcanoes stacked atop one another, with the youngest and largest, Fuji itself, forming over the Komitake and Ashitaka peaks. It is not just a cultural icon but also a popular destination for climbers and tourists, especially during the climbing season from July to early September, when thousands ascend daily. The symmetrical cone is a well-known symbol of Japan and is frequently depicted in art and photography, contributing to its status as a national symbol.

The Atacama Desert: Driest Place on Earth

The Atacama Desert, located in northern Chile, holds the distinction of being the driest desert in the world, with some parts receiving less than 1 millimeter of rainfall annually. Its extreme aridity is due to its positioning between two mountain chains (the Andes and the Chilean Coast Range) that effectively block moisture from both the Pacific and Atlantic oceans. The desert landscape is so Martian-like that it has been used by NASA to test instruments for Mars missions. Interestingly, despite its harsh conditions, the Atacama is home to over 500 species of flora, many of which are endemic, having adapted unique mechanisms to survive with minimal water. The desert also periodically experiences a phenomenon known as the "Desierto Florido" or "Flowering Desert," where, following rare and sporadic rainfall, the desert blooms with a variety of flowers in a vibrant display of life's resilience.

Iguazu Falls: A Natural Border

Iguazu Falls, located at the junction of Brazil, Argentina, and Paraguay, is one of the most spectacular waterfall systems in the world. This UNESCO World Heritage Site consists of approximately 275 individual waterfalls and cascades, with the number varying depending on the season. The name "Iguazu" originates from the Guarani or Tupi words 'y' [water] and 'ûasú [big], aptly describing the immense scale of these falls. Among the most awe-inspiring sections is the Devil's Throat, a U-shaped chasm that is 82 meters high, 150 meters wide, and 700 meters long. What makes Iguazu truly unique is not just its impressive size or beauty but also the fact that it can be viewed from three different countries, offering distinct perspectives from each nation's side of the falls.

Plitvice Lakes National Park: Cascading Beauty

Plitvice Lakes National Park in Croatia is celebrated for its distinctive chain of 16 terraced lakes, joined by waterfalls that extend into a limestone canyon. What makes these lakes truly unique is their dynamic range of vibrant colors, including azure, green, blue, and gray, which change constantly depending on the quantity of minerals or organisms in the water and the angle of sunlight. This natural phenomenon is due to tufa formations, which are created by the deposition of calcium carbonate from the flowing water, continually shaping and reshaping the waterfalls and barriers in the park. This ongoing geological process is a key feature of the park, making it a living, changing landscape that offers new sights and experiences over time. Recognized as a UNESCO World Heritage site, Plitvice Lakes is not only a stunning visual spectacle but also a prime example of nature's ability to sculpt breathtaking landscapes.

The Swiss Alps: Europe's Mountain Playground

The Swiss Alps are renowned not just for their picturesque landscapes but also for hosting the highest railway station in Europe. The Jungfraujoch station sits at an elevation of 3,454 meters (11,332 feet) above sea level, nestled between the Monch and Jungfrau mountains in the Bernese Alps. Known as the "Top of Europe," it offers visitors breathtaking views of the Aletsch Glacier, Europe's longest glacier, and serves as a gateway to a range of alpine activities. This railway station, accessible via a cogwheel train through a tunnel carved in the Eiger and Monch mountains, is a testament to Switzerland's pioneering feats in railway engineering and a hub for skiing, snowboarding, and hiking, drawing tourists seeking both adventure and scenic beauty year-round.

Lake Baikal: The World's Deepest Lake

Lake Baikal in Siberia is not only the world's deepest lake, reaching depths of 1,642 meters (5,387 feet), but it is also considered the oldest freshwater lake on Earth, estimated at 25 million years old. This massive lake contains about 20% of the world's unfrozen freshwater reserve, making it a crucial natural resource. Baikal's exceptional clarity and depth contribute to a unique ecosystem with thousands of plant and animal species, many of which are endemic, such as the Baikal seal. This high level of biodiversity has earned Lake Baikal the nickname "the Galápagos of Russia," highlighting its importance for both ecological study and conservation.

Uluru: Australia's Red Heart

Uluru, also known as Ayers Rock, is a massive sandstone monolith in the heart of the Northern Territory's arid "Red Centre" in Australia. Standing 348 meters (1,142 feet) high with a circumference of 9.4 kilometers (5.8 miles), Uluru is notable for appearing to change color at different times of the day and year, with sunset a particularly remarkable time when it briefly glows red. Uluru is deeply sacred to the Indigenous Anangu people, who have lived in the area for more than 10,000 years. The rock is adorned with various petroglyphs and is associated with numerous myths and legends in Anangu culture. In recognition of its cultural significance and natural beauty, climbing Uluru was officially banned in 2019, honoring the spiritual significance of the site to its traditional custodians.

Banff National Park: Canadian Rockies Gem

Banff National Park, established in 1885, is Canada's oldest national park and a jewel of the Canadian Rockies. Located in Alberta, the park spans 6,641 square kilometers of breathtaking mountainous terrain, renowned for its stunningly turquoise glacier-fed lakes, such as Lake Louise and Moraine Lake. These vibrant waters owe their striking color to rock flour, fine particles of rock ground by glacial movement, suspended in the water, which refract light. Banff's diverse ecosystem supports an array of wildlife, including grizzly bears, wolves, and bald eagles, making it not only a top destination for outdoor activities like hiking, skiing, and biking but also a vital area for wildlife conservation and natural studies.

Ha Long Bay: Vietnam's Limestone Marvel

Ha Long Bay, located in northeastern Vietnam, is a spectacular seascape sculpted during millions of years of geological evolution. The bay is famed for its approximately 1,600 limestone islands and islets, many of which rise dramatically from the water to form distinctive towering pillars. This UNESCO World Heritage site is steeped in mythological significance, with its name translating to "Bay of the Descending Dragon." Local legends say that the islands were created by a great dragon from the mountains, which charged towards the coast, its tail gouging out valleys and crevasses. As the dragon plunged into the sea, the areas dug up by its tail became filled with water, leaving only the high areas visible. Ha Long Bay is not only a place of breathtaking beauty but also a prime example of a landscape formed by both karst erosion and mythical storytelling.

The Namib Desert: Coastal Dunes and Desert Life

The Namib Desert, stretching along the coasts of Angola, Namibia, and South Africa, is one of the oldest deserts in the world, with an age estimated at between 55 and 80 million years. Renowned for its vast dune fields, which are among the tallest in the world, some dunes rise to over 300 meters (nearly 1000 feet). These striking sand formations are predominantly shaped by the strong onshore winds, and their rich red color comes from the high iron content of the sand, which oxidizes upon exposure to the air. The Namib is also home to a unique range of wildlife, including some species that are not found anywhere else in the world, such as the Namib desert beetle, which has developed the remarkable ability to harvest water from fog by condensing droplets on its bumpy back surface, demonstrating an extraordinary adaptation to the arid environment.

Komodo Island: Land of Dragons

Komodo Island in Indonesia is famously known as the home of the Komodo dragon, the largest living species of lizard, which can grow up to a formidable 3 meters (10 feet) in length and weigh as much as 70 kilograms (154 pounds). The island is part of Komodo National Park, which was established to protect these incredible creatures and their habitat. These dragons are apex predators and are known for their impressive hunting prowess, including their ability to take down animals as large as deer and water buffalo. Komodo dragons' unique physiology allows them to consume up to 80% of their body weight in a single meal, a crucial adaptation given the limited food resources in their arid island habitat. The island's rugged terrain, including its volcanic hillsides and dry forests, adds to the primordial allure of this ancient land of dragons.

The Blue Mountains: Australia's Natural Heritage

The Blue Mountains, located in New South Wales, Australia, are named for the natural blue haze that envelops them, a phenomenon resulting from the vast eucalyptus forests releasing droplets of oil into the air which, when combined with water vapor and sunlight, create the distinctive tinge. This region, a UNESCO World Heritage site, spans over 1 million hectares and features dramatic cliffs, deep forested valleys, and cascading water-falls. It's also known for the Three Sisters rock formation, which is steeped in Aboriginal legend and is one of the area's most photographed and iconic landmarks. The Blue Mountains offer a rich tapestry of bushland and conservation areas that host hundreds of species of flora and fauna, making it a crucial sanctuary for biodiversity and a favored destination for nature lovers and hikers worldwide.

Pamukkale: Turkey's Cotton Castle

Pamukkale, meaning "Cotton Castle" in Turkish, is a stunning natural wonder located in southwestern Turkey, famous for its white terraces formed by cascading thermal mineral waters rich in calcium carbonate. Over thousands of years, these flowing waters have hardened into natural pools and terraces, creating a surreal, snow-like landscape atop a hill. This geological phenomenon is not just a beautiful spectacle; the waters are believed to have therapeutic properties and have been used as a spa since the times of the ancient Romans. The site is also home to the ancient city of Hierapolis, established by the King of Pergamon in 190 BC, which adds historical depth to its visual appeal, making Pamukkale a fascinating blend of natural and archaeological heritage.

The Amazon River: The Mighty Waterway

The Amazon River, flowing across South America, is the largest river in the world by discharge volume of water. Notably, it was once believed to be the longest river in the world, but recent studies and measurements suggest that it is slightly shorter than the Nile. The Amazon pushes so much water into the Atlantic Ocean that it can alter the salinity of the ocean for up to 100 miles from its mouth. This mighty river runs through the Amazon Rainforest, housing an unparalleled biodiversity including approximately one-third of all known terrestrial species in the world. This immense ecosystem spans several countries and plays a critical role in the global climate by helping regulate atmospheric carbon levels.

The Maldives: A Tropical Paradise

The Maldives, an archipelago consisting of 1,192 coral islands grouped in 26 atolls in the Indian Ocean, is distinguished by its unique geography as the world's lowest-lying nation. With an average ground level elevation of just 1.5 meters above sea level, and the highest natural point being only 2.4 meters, the Maldives is particularly susceptible to rising sea levels due to climate change. The stunning natural beauty of its white-sand beaches, crystal-clear turquoise waters, and vibrant coral reefs make it a sought-after destination for tourists seeking a serene tropical getaway. Additionally, the Maldives' economy heavily relies on tourism and fishing, with the pristine condition of its coral reefs being vital for sustaining the local marine life that supports these industries.

The Matterhorn: A Swiss Icon

The Matterhorn, one of the most recognized mountains in the world for its pyramid-like shape, straddles the border between Switzerland and Italy. Standing at 4,478 meters (14,692 feet), it is one of the highest peaks in the Alps. The mountain's iconic shape has made it a classic symbol of the Swiss Alps and a coveted climb for mountaineers. The first successful ascent of the Matterhorn was achieved in 1865 by a team led by Edward Whymper, although the triumph was marred by tragedy when four members of the party fell to their deaths during the descent. This event marked a pivotal moment in the history of mountaineering, highlighting both the sport's inherent risks and its allure. The Matterhorn continues to attract thousands of climbers every year, drawn by its challenging routes and breathtaking scenery.

Kruger National Park: South Africa's Wildlife Haven

Kruger National Park, established in 1898, is one of South Africa's largest and most famous game reserves, encompassing nearly 2 million hectares. It offers one of the most diverse and abundant wildlife experiences in Africa, hosting a stunning variety of animals including the "Big Five": lions, leopards, rhinoceroses, elephants, and buffalos. This park is part of the Great Limpopo Transfrontier Park, a peace park that links Kruger with Gonarezhou National Park in Zimbabwe and Limpopo National Park in Mozambique. This collaboration allows wildlife to roam freely between the three sanctuaries. Kruger is not only a prime spot for biodiversity but also a leader in advanced environmental management techniques and policies, making it a pivotal area for conservation and a model for wildlife management around the world.

The Andes Mountains: South America's Backbone

The Andes Mountains form the longest continental mountain range in the world, stretching approximately 7,000 kilometers (4,350 miles) along the western coast of South

America through seven countries: Venezuela, Colombia, Ecuador, Peru, Bolivia, Chile, and Argentina. This immense range is also notable for containing the highest peak outside of Asia, Aconcagua, which rises 6,961 meters (22,838 feet) above sea level in Argentina. The Andes are not only pivotal in defining South America's geography but also its climate and ecosystems, creating rain shadows to the west and fostering rich biodiversity, including the unique cloud forests. These mountains have been vital to the cultural identity, agriculture, and economies of the Andean nations, influencing ancient civilizations like the Incas, who built one of the most extensive empires along its rugged terrain.

The Ring of Fire: Pacific Ocean's Volcanic Belt

The Ring of Fire is a major area in the basin of the Pacific Ocean where a large number of earthquakes and volcanic eruptions occur, forming a horseshoe-shaped belt that is approximately 40,000 kilometers (25,000 miles) long. It is associated with a nearly continuous series of oceanic trenches, volcanic arcs, and volcanic belts and plate movements. It contains over 75% of the world's active and dormant volcanoes and is also responsible for about 90% of the world's earthquakes, including some of the most catastrophic in human history. The Ring of Fire's intense seismic activity is not only a subject of continuous study but also a significant influence on the geology and climate of the surrounding regions, impacting millions of people who live in its vicinity.

The Richat Structure: Earth's Bullseye

The Richat Structure, also known as the Eye of the Sahara, is a prominent circular geological formation in the Sahara Desert near Ouadane, central Mauritania. Visible from space, this striking feature measures approximately 40 kilometers in diameter and was initially mistaken for a meteorite impact site. However, geological studies have since determined that it is a symmetrical uplift (dome) that has been eroded to expose the onion-like layers of rock. The Richat Structure is composed of sedimentary rock that has been deeply eroded by wind and water, revealing a range of rock types from different geologic periods. This geological marvel, now understood to be the result of natural geological processes, continues to be a subject of scientific study and a visual landmark for astronauts in orbit.

The Danube Delta: Europe's Wildlife Refuge

The Danube Delta, located in Eastern Europe where the Danube River meets the Black Sea, is the second largest river delta in Europe and one of the continent's most biodiverse regions. It spans across parts of Romania and Ukraine, covering more than 4,180 square kilometers of rivers, canals, marshes, and lakes. This vast wetland is home to over 300 species of birds and supports the largest reed bed ecosystems in the world. Among its notable residents are the Dalmatian pelicans and numerous other species of migratory birds, making it a vital bird sanctuary and a UNESCO World Heritage site. The delta's rich ecosystems also support a wide range of fish species, including sturgeons which are famous for producing caviar, underlining the delta's ecological as well as economic importance.

Raja Ampat: Indonesia's Coral Kingdom

Raja Ampat, located off the northwest tip of Bird's Head Peninsula on the island of New Guinea, in Indonesia's West Papua province, is often considered one of the world's richest marine biodiversity hotspots. The archipelago encompasses over 1,500 small islands and cays, featuring one of the richest coral reef ecosystems on earth. It is home to more than 1,300 species of coral reef fish, 600 species of hard coral, and represents about 75% of all known coral species, making it a prime location for diving and marine research. The incredible underwater scenery and the vast number of species found in Raja Ampat have earned it the nickname "The Last Paradise on Earth." This area plays a crucial role in the Coral Triangle, known for its extreme marine biodiversity and vital to global marine health.

The Gobi Desert: Asia's Expansive Wilderness

The Gobi Desert, stretching across northern China and southern Mongolia, is known as one of the world's largest deserts and a significant historical region, once part of the great Mongol Empire and a crucial segment of the Silk Road. Contrary to the typical sandy image of deserts, much of the Gobi is not sandy but is covered with bare rock and sparse vegetation, adapted to its extreme temperature fluctuations, which can swing from -40 degrees Celsius in winter to over 45 degrees Celsius in summer. The Gobi is also famous for its paleontological significance, as it has been a prime site for discovering well-preserved dinosaur fossils, including the first dinosaur eggs ever found, contributing greatly to our understanding of prehistoric life.

Table Mountain: Cape Town's Majestic Backdrop

Table Mountain, a prominent landmark overlooking Cape Town, South Africa, is distinguished by its flat top, which gives the mountain its name. This iconic plateau is approximately 3 kilometers from side to side and flanked by impressive cliffs, providing a dramatic backdrop to the city. The mountain is part of Table Mountain National Park and is home to over 1,500 species of plants, making it one of the richest floral regions globally and a part of the Cape Floral Kingdom. Remarkably, Table Mountain's plant diversity exceeds that of the entire United Kingdom. It also features a cableway that takes visitors to the summit, offering stunning views of Cape Town, the nearby peaks, and the surrounding ocean. Table Mountain is not only a significant tourist attraction but also a vital conservation area.

The Pantanal: Brazil's Wetland Wonderland

The Pantanal, sprawling across Brazil, Bolivia, and Paraguay, is the world's largest tropical wetland area and one of the most preserved, covering over 170,000 square kilometers during the wet season. This ecological treasure houses an incredibly dense array of biodiversity and is known for its spectacular wildlife viewing. It supports around 1000 bird species, 400 fish species, 300 mammalian species, and 480 reptile species. The Pantanal is especially renowned for being one of the best places to view jaguars in the wild. Additionally, it plays a crucial role in the hydrological cycle of the region, acting as a vast floodplain that absorbs and gradually releases water, helping to maintain the ecological balance of the area.

Mount Roraima: A Tepui's Mystical Summit

Mount Roraima, located on the triple border between Venezuela, Brazil, and Guyana, is one of the oldest geological formations on Earth, dating back about two billion years. This striking tepui (table-top mountain) rises 2,810 meters (9,220 feet) above sea level and is often shrouded in clouds. The flat summit covers roughly 31 square kilometers and is encircled by sheer 400-meter high cliffs, creating an isolated world with a unique ecosystem. The plateau is home to many endemic species of flora and fauna that are not found anywhere else on Earth, such as the carnivorous pitcher plant. The surreal, otherworldly landscape of Mount Roraima has inspired various myths and stories, including Arthur Conan Doyle's novel "The Lost World," where dinosaurs and other prehistoric creatures still roam.

The Okavango Delta: Botswana's Inland Oasis

The Okavango Delta in Botswana is one of the world's largest inland deltas, and unlike most river systems, it does not flow into the sea or ocean. Instead, the Okavango River empties onto open land, flooding the savanna and creating a unique and dynamic wetland that supports a diverse ecosystem. This annual flooding from the river occurs during the dry season, providing a critical source of water to the region's wildlife when other water sources are at their lowest. This phenomenon creates a lush animal habitat that supports a rich diversity of wildlife including elephants, lions, rhinos, and leopards, as well as over 400 species of birds. The delta's intricate pattern of channels, lagoons, and islands are shaped by the sediment deposited during these seasonal floods, constantly reshaping this vibrant landscape.

The Chocolate Hills: Philippines' Geological Wonder

The Chocolate Hills of Bohol, Philippines, are a prime example of a fascinating geological formation consisting of at least 1,260 hills, but there can be as many as 1,776 hills spread over an area of more than 50 square kilometers. These hills are covered in green grass that turns brown during the dry season, giving them the appearance of endless rows of chocolate kisses, hence their name. The origin of the Chocolate Hills is still a subject of debate among geologists, with theories including weathered rock formations and uplifted coral deposits. This peculiar and striking landscape is not only a famous tourist attraction but also a cultural icon of the Philippines, featured in the provincial flag and seal to symbolize the abundance of natural attractions in the region.

Zhangjiajie National Forest Park: China's Pillar Forest

Zhangjiajie National Forest Park in Hunan Province, China, is renowned for its breathtaking landscape of over 3,000 vertical pillars, each hundreds of meters tall, formed through physical erosion by expanding ice in the winter and the abundant vegetation covering the area. This remarkable topography is often shrouded in mist, adding an ethereal quality that has inspired artists and filmmakers, notably influencing the Hallelujah Mountains in James Cameron's film "Avatar." The park itself is part of the larger Wulingyuan Scenic Area, a UNESCO World Heritage Site since 1992, which is celebrated for its pristine natural beauty and the diversity of its plant and wildlife, including several endangered species. Zhangjiajie's dramatic scenery is also complemented by its rich cultural heritage, home to the Tujia, Miao, and Bai ethnic groups, making it a significant cultural and natural marvel.

The Southern Alps: New Zealand's Mountain Range

The Southern Alps, extending almost the length of New Zealand's South Island, are the backbone of the island and a climatic divider. This major mountain range includes Aoraki/Mount Cook, New Zealand's highest peak at 3,724 meters (12,218 feet). Remarkably, the range is still rising due to tectonic pressures as the Pacific and Indo-Australian Plates collide. The force of this ongoing uplift counteracts the high rates of erosion caused by the heavy rainfalls the mountains receive, estimated at up to 10 meters of uplift over 1000 years. This dynamic geological activity not only shapes the breathtaking landscapes of the Southern Alps but also contributes to the frequent earthquakes experienced in the region. The range is also a hub for adventure tourism, offering opportunities for skiing, mountaineering, and scenic flights.

Chapter Seven
Historical Hoaxes

The Piltdown Man: A Prehistoric Fake

The Piltdown Man stands as one of the most infamous scientific hoaxes in history, initially touted as a critical missing link in human evolution. Discovered in 1912 by amateur archaeologist Charles Dawson in Piltdown, England, the fragments of a skull and jawbone were presented as evidence of a previously unknown early human, Eoanthropus dawsoni. The scientific community was divided over the find until 1953, when new dating technology and further analysis revealed that the bones were a deliberate forgery, combining a medieval human skull with the 500-year-old lower jaw of an orangutan and filed-down teeth. The exposure of the hoax not only embarrassed the scientific community but also significantly impacted the study of human evolution by misleading researchers for over 40 years. The true identity of the forger remains unknown, adding a layer of mystery to the cautionary tale of the Piltdown Man.

The Cardiff Giant: America's Petrified Man

The Cardiff Giant, one of the most famous hoaxes in American history, was a 10-foot-tall purported "petrified man" unearthed in 1869 on a farm in Cardiff, New York. The giant was actually a statue sculpted from a block of gypsum and artificially aged to appear ancient. It was created by New York tobacconist George Hull, who orchestrated the hoax after a heated argument over Biblical giants. Hull hoped to not only fool the public but also to mock religious fundamentalists who believed in literal interpretations of such tales.

Upon its discovery, the Cardiff Giant became a sensation, drawing thousands of curious spectators and charging admission fees. The hoax was eventually exposed, but not before Hull made a substantial profit from his elaborate ruse. The Cardiff Giant still holds a place in folklore as a symbol of gullible consumerism and sensationalist journalism.

The War of the Worlds Broadcast

The War of the Worlds broadcast on October 30, 1938, is one of the most famous radio broadcasts in history due to its realistic portrayal of a Martian invasion, which reportedly caused widespread panic among listeners. Directed and narrated by Orson Welles, the broadcast was a radio adaptation of H.G. Wells' novel "The War of the Worlds." Despite disclaimers at the beginning and during the broadcast stating it was fictional, many listeners tuned in late and, in the context of the looming threat of World War II, believed the events were real. This broadcast dramatically demonstrated the power of the media and has been studied extensively in discussions about mass communication and the psychology of panic. The event also catapulted Orson Welles to fame, showcasing his innovative use of radio as a medium for storytelling.

The Great Moon Hoax of 1835

The Great Moon Hoax of 1835 was a series of articles published by "The New York Sun," a popular newspaper, claiming that life and even civilization had been discovered on the Moon. The articles, written by reporter Richard Adams Locke, purportedly based on observations made by Sir John Herschel, a famous astronomer of the time, detailed fantastical creatures and environments. These included human-bat hybrids, unicorns, and lush landscapes. The series was intended as satire against more outlandish journalistic practices of the era, but it was taken seriously by many readers, boosting the newspaper's circulation dramatically. The hoax was revealed weeks later, showing the gullibility of the public and the power of the press, and it remains one of the most famous media hoaxes in history.

The Hitler Diaries Scandal

The Hitler Diaries scandal in 1983 is one of the most notorious cases of forgery in journalism. The German magazine "Stern" believed it had obtained the personal diaries of Adolf Hitler, which were supposedly discovered in wreckage from a plane crash in East Germany. These diaries, claimed to have been written between 1932 and 1945, were in fact fabricated by Konrad Kujau, a Stuttgart-based forger and antiques dealer. Kujau had skillfully aged and filled 60 volumes with supposed insights into Hitler's daily life and thoughts. "Stern" paid millions for the diaries, and the story made international headlines when excerpts were published, even before their authenticity was verified. However, forensic experts soon determined that the diaries were written with materials not available during the alleged time period, unraveling one of the most embarrassing episodes in media history. The incident served as a stark reminder of the importance of verification in journalism.

The Loch Ness Monster Photo

The Loch Ness Monster, affectionately known as "Nessie," is primarily known through the iconic 1934 photograph known as the "Surgeon's Photo," which seemed to show the monster's long neck emerging from the waters of Loch Ness in Scotland. This image cemented Nessie as a cultural sensation and sparked worldwide interest in the creature. However, decades later, it was revealed to be a hoax. The photo was actually staged using a toy submarine fitted with a sea-serpent head, concocted by Marmaduke Wetherell, a disgruntled movie maker who sought to embarrass the newspaper that had ridiculed his earlier claims about Nessie. This revelation, though it debunked the most famous evidence of Nessie's existence, did little to dampen the public's fascination with the legendary creature.

The Crop Circle Phenomenon

Crop circles, intricate patterns that appear overnight in fields of crops such as wheat, barley, and corn, have fascinated and puzzled observers since they gained widespread attention in the late 1970s. While initially thought to be the work of extraterrestrial beings, it was later revealed that many of these formations were created by humans as elaborate pranks. The phenomenon was first popularized by two British men, Doug Bower and Dave Chorley, who in 1991 confessed to making hundreds of crop circles over the preceding decades using simple tools like planks of wood, ropes, and wire. Their motive was to stir up local folklore and UFO stories. Despite this revelation, crop circles continue to be a global phenomenon with many new formations attributed to artists and imitators who create elaborate designs, often overnight, to intrigue or carry on the tradition.

The Donation of Constantine

The Donation of Constantine was a document purportedly written by Emperor Constantine the Great, wherein he transferred authority over Rome and the western part of the Roman Empire to the Pope. For centuries, this document significantly influenced the political and religious landscape of medieval Europe, bolstering the papal claim to temporal power. However, it was proven to be a forgery in the 15th century by Lorenzo Valla, a Renaissance humanist and philologist, through linguistic and textual analysis. Valla demonstrated that the Latin used in the document did not match the Latin that would have been used during Constantine's era, highlighting anachronisms that could only belong to a later period. This critical examination not only marked a significant moment in philological studies but also shifted the balance of power between the papacy and the secular rulers of Europe.

The Fortsas Bibliohoax

The Fortsas Bibliohoax of 1840 is a notable episode in literary history, involving a fictional auction of rare books that captured the attention of bibliophiles across Europe. A man named Count Johann Nepomuk von Fortsas, who was entirely fictitious, was claimed to have amassed a collection of books of which each was said to be the sole copy in existence. Invitations were sent to renowned book collectors and libraries to attend this auction in the small Belgian town of Binche. On the day of the supposed auction, buyers arrived only to discover that there was no such count, no book collection, and that the entire setup was a hoax orchestrated by a local antiquarian and bibliophile, Renier Hubert Ghislain Chalon, as a prank to satirize and critique the absurd lengths to which collectors would go for rare books. The event remains a humorous and enlightening tale about the nature of collectors' obsessions and gullibility.

The Dihydrogen Monoxide Hoax

The Dihydrogen Monoxide (DHMO) hoax is a well-known scientific prank that highlights how the use of scientific terminology can create misleading perceptions. Dihydrogen monoxide is simply water, but when described using a chemical name that sounds unfamiliar and potentially hazardous, it can seem dangerous. Proponents of the hoax claim that DHMO is a colorless, odorless chemical that can cause severe burns in its gaseous state (steam), is used as an industrial solvent and coolant, and is found in biopsies of pre-cancerous cells, leading to alarm and misunderstanding. This hoax, which has circulated since the 1990s, often includes calls to ban DHMO and serves as a lesson in critical thinking and the importance of scientific literacy, demonstrating how easily scientific facts can be manipulated to create fear.

The Fiji Mermaid: Barnum's Aquatic Marvel

The Fiji Mermaid was one of P.T. Barnum's most famous and deceptive attractions, showcased in the 1840s as a genuine mermaid. In reality, it was a grotesque fabrication, cleverly constructed from the upper body and head of a monkey sewn onto the back half of a fish, likely a salmon. The concoction was then dried, preserving it in a way that gave it a creepy, mummified appearance. Barnum's promotion of this curiosity as a real mermaid successfully drew in huge crowds, eager to see this mythical creature. The Fiji Mermaid became a quintessential example of Barnum's ability to exploit public curiosity and gullibility, cementing his reputation as a master of showmanship and spectacle in the burgeoning world of American entertainment.

The Giant's Causeway: Nature's Hoax

The Giant's Causeway, located on the northeast coast of Northern Ireland, is an area of about 40,000 interlocking basalt columns, the result of an ancient volcanic fissure eruption. What makes the Giant's Causeway particularly fascinating is the uniformity and hexagonal shape of the columns, which look so precise that they could be mistaken as the handiwork of an industrious giant, as local legends suggest. According to myth, the causeway was built by the Irish giant Fionn mac Cumhaill (Finn McCool) as a pathway to Scotland to confront his Scottish rival. Geologically speaking, these structures were formed about 50 to 60 million years ago when molten lava cooled rapidly, contracting and fracturing in a way that formed the mostly hexagonal columns seen today. This UNESCO World Heritage Site not only showcases an incredible natural phenomenon but also captures the imagination with its mythic origins.

The Alien Autopsy Film

The Alien Autopsy film, which surfaced in 1995, purported to show the medical dissection of an alien body recovered from the supposed crash of a flying saucer near Roswell, New Mexico, in 1947. Presented by London-based entrepreneur Ray Santilli, the film caused a media frenzy and was broadcast in more than 30 countries, reigniting UFO conspiracy theories worldwide. However, it was later revealed to be a hoax. Santilli admitted in 2006 that the film was not authentic but rather a staged reconstruction of an alleged original film he had viewed in the 1990s, which had deteriorated beyond recovery. The "autopsy" was actually performed on a fabricated alien, constructed by special effects artist John Humphreys, a professional sculptor and animatronics expert, using materials such as animal organs and latex.

The Drake's Plate of Brass: A Historical Puzzle

The Drake's Plate of Brass is a notorious historical puzzle, long considered a significant artifact from the 16th century, allegedly left by the English explorer Sir Francis Drake during his 1579 landing on the coast of California. The plate was purported to be Drake's claim to the territory on behalf of England. However, the mystery surrounding the plate escalated when it was discovered in 1936, as it soon became a subject of intense debate among historians. Decades later, in the 1970s, scientific analysis finally revealed that the plate was a modern forgery, created by a group of local historians in the early 20th century as part of a practical joke. This revelation turned the once-valued artifact into a classic example of a historical hoax, showcasing the intricacies of archaeological forgeries and their impact on historical narratives.

The Tasaday Tribe

The Tasaday tribe, which gained international attention in the 1970s, was initially presented as a "Stone Age" tribe living in complete isolation in the rainforests of Mindanao,

Philippines. This discovery, promoted by government anthropologist Manuel Elizalde, fascinated the world with claims of a pure and untouched society. However, subsequent investigations in the early 1980s raised significant doubts about the authenticity of the tribe's isolation and primitive status. Critics argued that the Tasaday were actually local tribespeople dressed up and manipulated into acting primitively, casting the entire scenario as a potential hoax designed to attract media attention and conservation funding. Later reassessments suggested a more nuanced picture, indicating that while the Tasaday indeed might have been more isolated than typical modern societies, their portrayal had been exaggerated, highlighting the complexities involved in understanding and representing indigenous cultures.

The Berners Street Hoax: London's Day of Chaos

The Berners Street Hoax, orchestrated by Theodore Hook in 1810, created a day of chaos on Berners Street in London. Hook, a notorious practical joker, made a bet with his friend Samuel Beazley that he could transform any house in London into the most talked-about address in a single week. To win the bet, Hook sent out thousands of letters in the name of Mrs. Tottenham, the resident of 54 Berners Street, requesting deliveries, visitors, and assistance. On the appointed day, a bewildered Mrs. Tottenham watched as a slew of tradesmen, dignitaries, and even the Lord Mayor of London arrived at her door. The street was soon in utter chaos, packed with crowds and carriages, making it impossible for anyone to pass. The prank not only succeeded in disrupting the city but also remains one of the most elaborate and effective practical jokes in history, illustrating Hook's clever manipulation of social mechanisms of the time.

The Mechanical Turk: An Illusion of Intelligence

The Mechanical Turk was an ingenious 18th-century invention by Wolfgang von Kempelen, presented in 1770 as a chess-playing automaton capable of defeating human opponents. This mechanical marvel appeared to be a life-sized figure dressed in Turkish attire, seated behind a large wooden cabinet, with a chessboard placed on top. Audiences were astounded as the Turk, supposedly a self-operating machine, played and often won against skilled human chess players, including famous figures like Napoleon Bonaparte and Benjamin Franklin. However, the true nature of the Turk was a clever deception:

a hidden human chess master was inside the cabinet, controlling the movements of the mechanical arm. The Mechanical Turk remained a popular spectacle for decades, serving as an early exploration of the theme of artificial intelligence in the pre-digital age, and later inspiring the name of Amazon's crowdsourcing platform, Amazon Mechanical Turk.

The Disappearance of Richard Colvin Cox

The disappearance of Richard Colvin Cox in 1950 is one of the most intriguing mysteries in U.S. military history. A second-year cadet at the United States Military Academy at West Point, Cox vanished without a trace after last being seen in the company of a man known only as "George." Despite extensive searches and investigations, including efforts by the FBI, no conclusive evidence has ever been found regarding his fate. His disappearance prompted widespread media attention and numerous theories, ranging from abduction and espionage to voluntary disappearance. To this day, Cox's case remains officially unsolved, making it one of the few instances of a West Point cadet mysteriously disappearing, leaving behind a lasting legacy of mystery and speculation.

The Great Stock Exchange Fraud of 1814

The Great Stock Exchange Fraud of 1814 was a remarkable scheme perpetrated by Lord Cochrane and others to manipulate the London stock market. The fraudsters spread false news of Napoleon Bonaparte's death, which led to a surge in British government securities. On February 21, 1814, a man dressed as a French officer landed in Dover, proclaiming that Napoleon had been defeated. The news spread rapidly to London, significantly boosting British government securities. When the truth emerged that the news was entirely fabricated, the market crashed, and the perpetrators were caught. Lord Cochrane was convicted and sentenced for his role in the hoax, though he always maintained his innocence. This scandal is one of the most infamous examples of stock market manipulation in history, showing the vulnerability of financial markets to rumors and fake news.

The Pied Piper of Hamelin: A Legend with Truth?

The Pied Piper of Hamelin is a legend originating from a small town in Germany, chronicled as early as the 13th century, involving a mysterious figure who rid the town of rats by luring them away with his magical flute. When the townspeople refused to pay for his service, he used his instrument to lead their children away, never to be seen again. Intriguingly, historians believe that this tale could be based on real events, suggesting that the children's disappearance might symbolize the emigration or mass recruitment of young locals to settle in Eastern Europe. Records from Hamelin itself refer to a stained glass church window, created around 1300, which depicted the Piper, affirming the legend's deep roots in local history and culture. This blending of folklore and potential historical fact contributes to the enduring fascination with the Pied Piper's tale.

The Spaghetti Tree Hoax

The Spaghetti Tree Hoax is one of the most celebrated April Fool's Day pranks ever conducted by the BBC, specifically on its current affairs program "Panorama" on April 1, 1957. The broadcast featured a segment showing a Swiss family purportedly harvesting spaghetti from their family "spaghetti tree." At the time, spaghetti was relatively unknown in the UK, and many Britons were unfamiliar with how it was produced. Narrated by distinguished broadcaster Richard Dimbleby, the segment showed women carefully plucking strands of spaghetti from tree branches and laying them in the sun to dry. This convincing portrayal led many viewers to believe the fabricated story, with some even contacting the BBC for advice on growing their own spaghetti trees. The hoax capitalized on the public's unfamiliarity with the food and has since been hailed as a classic example of television satire.

The Paul is Dead Conspiracy

The "Paul is Dead" conspiracy is one of the most bizarre and enduring legends in the history of rock music, originating in 1969. It claimed that Paul McCartney, of the Beatles, had died in a car crash in 1966 and was secretly replaced by a look-alike. Fans cited supposed "clues" found in the lyrics and artwork of Beatles albums, including the infamous Abbey Road album cover where Paul is barefoot and out of step with the other members, symbolizing a corpse in a funeral procession according to believers. The rumor gained such traction that McCartney himself took to the media to debunk it, humorously noting that if he were dead, he would be the last to know. This conspiracy theory has been the subject of much discussion and analysis, contributing to the lore surrounding the Beatles while highlighting the phenomenon of fan-driven mythologies in popular culture.

The Roswell UFO Incident: A Government Cover-Up?

The Roswell UFO Incident of 1947 is a seminal event in UFO folklore, where debris from a mysterious object was recovered near Roswell, New Mexico. Initially reported by the local Army Air Force base as a "flying disc," the military soon retracted the statement, claiming the debris was merely a conventional weather balloon. This switch sparked decades of conspiracy theories, alleging a government cover-up of an alien spacecraft crash. The incident's intrigue deepened in the 1990s when the U.S. military disclosed that the debris was part of a classified project called "Mogul," involving high-altitude balloons to monitor Soviet nuclear tests. Despite this explanation, the debate over whether it was a cover-up or a misidentified military experiment continues to fuel speculation and a significant UFO subculture around Roswell.

The Ossian Poems

The Ossian Poems, presented by Scottish poet James Macpherson in the 1760s, were initially celebrated as translations of ancient epic poems written by Ossian, a supposed Gaelic bard from the 3rd century. Macpherson's works, including "Fingal" and "Temora," captivated readers with their romantic depictions of the Scottish Highlands and deeply influenced the emerging Romantic movement in literature across Europe. However, controversy soon arose regarding their authenticity. Critics, most notably literary giant Dr. Samuel Johnson, accused Macpherson of fabricating the poems, leading to a heated public debate. Despite Macpherson's persistent claims of translating from ancient sources, he never produced the original manuscripts, and subsequent scholarly analysis suggested that the poems were more likely his own creations, heavily based on Gaelic folklore. This controversy did not detract from their impact; the poems influenced many notable writers and poets, including Goethe and the young Walter Scott.

The Persian Princess Mummy

The Persian Princess is the name given to an alleged mummy discovered in Pakistan in October 2000 that was initially believed to be the remains of an ancient Persian princess dating back 2,600 years. The mummy surfaced in the antiquities black market, sparking immediate international interest due to its rarity as mummies are not traditionally associated with ancient Persian culture. However, upon examination, experts quickly raised concerns about its authenticity. The "princess" turned out to be a modern forgery, cleverly constructed using a mixture of ancient and modern materials, including a dental filling and modern glues observed in the wrappings. Tragically, it was later revealed through carbon dating and other forensic techniques that the mummy was actually the body of a young woman from the late 20th century, likely a recent murder victim, adding a grim chapter to the story of this supposed archaeological find. This case underscored the dark side of the illicit antiquities trade and the ethical complexities surrounding archaeological artifacts.

The Hollow Earth Theory

The Hollow Earth Theory is a fascinating and peculiar hypothesis that dates back to the 17th century, suggesting that the planet Earth is entirely hollow or contains a substantial interior space. Notably championed by Edmond Halley in 1692, the theory proposed that Earth might consist of several concentric shells and even a central core that could be inhabited. Halley suggested that this could explain anomalous compass readings, proposing the existence of an atmospheric layer inside the Earth that could support life. Over the centuries, this idea inspired a variety of scientific and literary works, including Jules Verne's famous novel "Journey to the Center of the Earth." While modern science has debunked the Hollow Earth Theory through geological data and the study of Earth's seismology, it remains a popular subject in works of fiction and conspiracy theories.

The Mummy of King Tut's Curse

The curse of King Tutankhamun, often referred to as "King Tut's Curse," is a legendary warning purported to harm those who disturb the young pharaoh's tomb. Discovered in 1922 by Howard Carter in the Valley of the Kings, the tomb was rumored to bear an inscription that read, "Death shall come on swift wings to him who disturbs the peace of the king." Although no such inscription has been found, the deaths of several members of the excavation team and associated individuals shortly after the tomb's opening fueled widespread public fascination with the curse. The most notable of these was the death of Lord Carnarvon, the financial backer of the excavation, who died under mysterious circumstances in Cairo shortly after the tomb was opened. Media coverage and public intrigue linked these events to the supposed curse, blending fact with fiction and cementing the legend in popular culture. Modern analyses suggest that mold spores or bacteria in the tomb could have caused some illnesses, but the curse itself remains a myth rooted more in folklore than in actual danger.

The Turin Papyrus Map Hoax

The Turin Papyrus Map, often misunderstood due to its rare and ancient origin, is actually not a hoax but rather one of the oldest known geological and topographical maps from ancient Egypt, dated to around 1150 BCE during the reign of Ramesses IV. This map details the quarrying expedition to the Wadi Hammamat in Eastern Egypt, which was famous for its bekhen-stone (a type of sandstone) and gold. The papyrus shows a 15-kilometer stretch of Wadi Hammamat, indicating the locations of mountains, roads, and water sources with annotations that provide insight into the logistical aspects of the mining expedition. This ancient document is not only a significant historical artifact but also a testament to the early Egyptians' skills in geography and resource management, debunking any notions of it being a modern-day forgery or hoax.

John Dillinger's Face

John Dillinger, the infamous American bank robber during the early 1930s, famously attempted to alter his appearance to evade law enforcement. In 1934, as the FBI closed in on his criminal activities, Dillinger underwent plastic surgery to transform his well-known face and even tried to remove his fingerprints with acid. The surgeries included changes to his facial features such as his chin and cheeks and were performed crudely, causing him significant pain and resulting in a somewhat distorted appearance. Despite these drastic efforts, Dillinger was recognized and ultimately killed by FBI agents outside the Biograph Theater in Chicago, just a few months after his procedures. His attempt at altering his appearance is often cited as one of the early instances of criminal plastic surgery.

The Fairy Ring Phenomenon

The fairy ring phenomenon is a natural occurrence where a ring or arc of mushrooms appears in grassy areas, often associated with folklore and myths. Scientifically, these rings are formed by the outward growth of a fungal organism below the surface of the ground, which starts from a single point and grows outward. As the fungus grows, it consumes nutrients in the soil, causing the mushrooms to emerge at the edges of the expanding circle. Over time, the center of the circle depletes its nutrients and dies off, leaving the ring shape. These rings can continue to grow for many years, expanding outward as long as soil conditions remain favorable. Some fairy rings are known to have diameters larger than 10 meters, illustrating the impressive and extensive underground network of these fungi.

Mummy Wheat

"Mummy wheat" refers to an archaeological myth popularized in the 19th century, claiming that seeds found in ancient Egyptian tombs, allegedly thousands of years old, could still germinate. The myth was fueled by stories of seeds found in such tombs being planted and sprouting, suggesting extraordinary longevity. It sparked a brief craze among Europeans and Americans who sought these seeds as curiosities and for agricultural experiments. However, scientific testing eventually debunked this myth, demonstrating that seeds of such great age could not remain viable, especially under conditions typical of those found in tombs. The supposed germination was likely due to contamination with modern seeds, and today, "mummy wheat" is cited as a classic example of pseudoscience in archaeology.

The Fountain of Youth: Ponce de León's Quest

The Fountain of Youth, a legendary spring reputed to restore the youth of anyone who drinks or bathes in its waters, is closely associated with the Spanish explorer Juan Ponce de León. According to popular myth, Ponce de León discovered Florida in 1513 while searching for this mystical water source. However, modern historians have largely debunked this story as a myth; there is no evidence from his time that Ponce de León was actually looking for the Fountain of Youth during his explorations. Instead, this tale was likely attached to his name by later writers. The legend persists in popular culture, symbolizing the human desire for renewal and eternal youth, and continues to draw tourists to St. Augustine, Florida, where a site claimed to be the Fountain of Youth has been a visitor attraction since the 19th century.

The Amityville: A Haunted House Tale

The Amityville Horror story, which captures the chilling tale of the Lutz family's brief residence at 112 Ocean Avenue in Amityville, New York, became famous worldwide following the publication of Jay Anson's 1977 book. The narrative centers around the claim that the Lutz family experienced numerous supernatural phenomena, including strange noises, mysterious odors, and levitating objects, after moving into a home where Ronald DeFeo Jr. had murdered six members of his family in 1974. Skeptics and several investigations have since suggested that the haunting was a hoax, greatly exaggerated to gain media attention and profit. Despite doubts about its veracity, the story has spawned a series of books, documentaries, and a successful film franchise, entrenching the Amityville house as one of the most famous haunted house stories in American pop culture.

The Cottingley Fairies: Enchanted Photographs

The Cottingley Fairies saga began in 1917 when two young cousins, Elsie Wright and Frances Griffiths, claimed to have photographed fairies near their home in Cottingley, England. The photographs, showing the girls with ethereal fairy figures, captured the public's imagination and even convinced Sir Arthur Conan Doyle, the creator of Sherlock Holmes and a spiritualist, of their authenticity. He published the photos in a 1920 article, arguing they were clear evidence of psychic phenomena. However, in 1983, the cousins confessed that the photographs were fabricated using cardboard cutouts of fairies, although Frances maintained that they had indeed seen fairies. The episode remains a notable example of how easily elaborate hoaxes can be constructed and the willingness of even the intelligent and educated to believe in the fantastical.

The Native of Formosa

The Native of Formosa hoax, orchestrated by George Psalmanazar in the early 18th century, is one of the most audacious frauds in literary history. Psalmanazar, a Frenchman, claimed to be the first native of Formosa (modern-day Taiwan) to visit Europe. With a convincing story, complete with a fake language, customs, and a detailed description of the island, he managed to fool many in London, including prominent intellectuals of the Royal Society. He published a book, "An Historical and Geographical Description of Formosa," which was initially a success due to public curiosity about exotic lands. His deception included religious rituals, a Formosan calendar, and even samples of an invented Formosan language. Psalmanazar's hoax was eventually exposed, yet he remained in England and later repented, confessing the deceit in his autobiography, which ironically gained him some respect for its honesty.

The Great Wall of China Spacewalk Hoax

In 2008, a photograph allegedly showing a Chinese astronaut walking in space with the Great Wall of China visible below circulated widely on the internet and in various media outlets. This image fueled the longstanding myth that the Great Wall is visible from space with the naked eye. However, the photo was quickly debunked as a hoax. In reality, while the Great Wall can be seen from space, it is barely discernible under specific conditions, such as favorable lighting and clear weather, and definitely not at the scale or clarity depicted in the viral image. The hoax underscored the ease with which digital images can be manipulated and the rapid spread of misinformation in the digital age, especially when it plays into popular myths or national pride.

The Jersey Devil: A Cryptid Legend

The Jersey Devil is a legendary creature said to inhabit the Pine Barrens of Southern New Jersey, with tales of its existence dating back to the 18th century. Described as a flying biped with hooves, the origins of the Jersey Devil legend stem from a tale about a local woman named Mother Leeds who, upon finding out she was pregnant with her 13th child, cursed it, declaring it would be the devil. The child was born normal but supposedly transformed into a monstrous creature, flying up the chimney and into the barrens. Over the centuries, this cryptid has become a prominent feature of local folklore, blamed for various livestock killings and strange noises in the night. It's also been embraced as a quirky part of New Jersey culture, inspiring sports team names, outdoor guides, and various merchandise.

The Awful Disclosures of Maria Monk

"The Awful Disclosures of Maria Monk, or, The Hidden Secrets of a Nun's Life in a Convent Exposed" was published in 1836 and quickly became a bestseller, feeding into the anti-Catholic sentiment prevalent in the United States at the time. Maria Monk claimed to have escaped from the Hôtel-Dieu convent in Montreal, where she was allegedly subjected to horrific abuse and witnessed infanticide among other atrocities. The book caused a public uproar and intense scrutiny of Catholic convents. However, subsequent investigations revealed significant inconsistencies in her story, and it was eventually discredited as a fabrication. Monk's confessions were likely coached and exaggerated by nativist anti-Catholic groups using her story to further their political agenda, showcasing early instances of sensationalist journalism used to inflame public opinion.

The Chupacabra: A Modern Monster Myth

The Chupacabra, or "goat-sucker" in Spanish, is a creature of modern folklore first reported in Puerto Rico in the mid-1990s. It is said to prey on livestock, especially goats, leaving behind animals with strange puncture wounds and reportedly drained of blood. Initially described as a reptilian creature with spines along its back, subsequent sightings across the Americas have varied dramatically, with some descriptions resembling wild dogs or other more canine-like creatures suffering from mange. Despite numerous reported sightings, there is no scientific evidence to support the existence of the Chupacabra. Biologists and wildlife management officials typically attribute attacks on livestock to known, native predators and identify supposed Chupacabra specimens as coyotes, dogs, or other mammals afflicted by mange or other diseases, which alter their appearance and may provoke myths and misidentifications.

The De Sitter Hoax

The De Sitter Hoax refers to a prank played by physicist George Gamow and his colleagues in the early 20th century. They fabricated a telegram that was supposedly sent by the famous astronomer Willem de Sitter to the Mount Wilson Observatory, claiming that life had been discovered on the planet Mars. The telegram was initially taken seriously by many at the observatory and created quite a stir. The hoax was meant as a playful jab at the fervor of the time surrounding the possibility of extraterrestrial life, highlighted by the widespread interest in Percival Lowell's theories about Martian canals. This incident showcased the lighter side of some of the era's leading scientists and their willingness to poke fun at the sensationalism often surrounding astronomical discoveries.

The Philadelphia Experiment: A Naval Mystery

The Philadelphia Experiment is an alleged military experiment that supposedly occurred in 1943 at the Philadelphia Naval Shipyard. The story goes that the USS Eldridge, a naval destroyer escort, was rendered invisible, or "cloaked," to enemy devices. The origin of the tale involves claims of merging quantum and Einstein's unified field theories, and it supposedly led to severe physical effects on the crew members, some of whom, according to legend, suffered from grave mental and physical disturbances. Many believe the story to be a hoax, with no substantial evidence or corroborating witnesses, and the U.S. Navy has officially denied that the experiment ever took place. Despite its dubious authenticity, the story has fueled conspiracy theories and inspired various books, documentaries, and a 1984 feature film, cementing its place in the annals of American folklore.

Lobsang Rampa

Lobsang Rampa was the pen name of Cyril Henry Hoskin, a British plumber who claimed to be a Tibetan lama and authored several books on spiritual topics in the mid-20th century. His most famous work, "The Third Eye," published in 1956, purports to describe his experiences and training as a monk in a Tibetan monastery. Hoskin's books, filled with mystical and supposedly autobiographical tales, became bestsellers and significantly influenced Western perceptions of Tibetan Buddhism and the occult. However, it was later revealed that he had never been to Tibet and his real identity was that of an Englishman with no Buddhist training. Despite being exposed as a fraud, Rampa continued to write and maintain his Tibetan persona, and his works remain popular among readers interested in the mystical and esoteric.

The Nylon Stocking Color TV Hoax

In 1962, Swedish television successfully pranked its viewers by claiming that placing nylon stockings over their black-and-white TV screens would enable them to see broadcasts in color. The announcer explained that the mesh of the stockings would bend the light in a way that created the illusion of color images. Despite the implausibility, many viewers eagerly tried the trick, only to be disappointed when it didn't work. This April Fools' Day prank highlighted the gullibility of the public and the influential power of television.

The Patterson-Gimlin Bigfoot Film: A Cryptid Icon

The Patterson-Gimlin film, shot in 1967 in Northern California, remains one of the most compelling and debated pieces of visual evidence in the lore of Bigfoot, the North American cryptid. The film captures what appears to be a large, hairy, bipedal ape-like creature walking through a clearing, famously turning to look at the camera before disappearing into the woods. Shot by Roger Patterson and Bob Gimlin, the film has been subjected to numerous analyses by experts in various fields, from primatology to special effects. Despite extensive scrutiny, the authenticity of the film has never been definitively proven or debunked, making it a seminal artifact in cryptozoology and a cultural icon that has fueled the ongoing fascination with the legend of Bigfoot.

The Bathtub Hoax

The Bathtub Hoax is a famous journalistic prank pulled by H.L. Mencken, a noted American satirist and cultural critic, in 1917. Mencken published an article in the "New York Evening Mail" claiming that the bathtub was a relatively recent invention introduced into the United States in 1842, accompanied by a detailed and entirely fictitious history. He fabricated events, such as President Millard Fillmore installing the first bathtub in the White House, to add credibility and humorous historical context. The article was intended as a light-hearted commentary on the gullibility of the public and the absurdity of American puritanism. Surprisingly, the story was taken seriously by many readers and was subsequently cited as fact in other publications for years, demonstrating Mencken's point about the ease with which the public could be misled by the media.

The Tour of the World in Ten Days

In 1904, a clever ruse by a French newspaper captivated its audience with a series of articles about an entirely fictional competition: a challenge to circumnavigate the globe in just ten days. This imaginative hoax predated and perhaps inspired other fictional races and global adventures, like the well-known "The Race Around the World." The newspaper's detailed accounts and updates on the competitors' progress enthralled readers, many of whom followed the events with keen interest, unaware that they were tracking an entirely fabricated journey. This hoax not only entertained but also showcased the period's growing public fascination with rapid global travel and adventure, highlighting how easily the media could craft and spread engaging narratives that captured the collective imagination.

The Crystal Skulls: Mysterious Artifacts or Modern Fakes?

The Crystal Skulls are a series of skull-shaped artifacts made from quartz, purported by some to be ancient Mesoamerican relics with mystical properties. However, extensive examinations have cast significant doubt on these claims. Many of the known skulls first surfaced in the 19th and 20th centuries without clear documentation of their origins. Scientific analysis, including studies conducted by the British Museum and the Smithsonian Institution, has revealed that several of these skulls were likely crafted in the 19th century, using modern tools not available to ancient artisans. These findings suggest that the skulls are more likely to be fabrications, possibly intended as curiosities or hoaxes, rather than authentic pre-Columbian artifacts. Despite this, the crystal skulls have captivated the public imagination, featuring prominently in New Age mysticism and popular culture, including being the focal point of *Indiana Jones and the Kingdom of the Crystal Skull* (2008)

Debunking Uri Geller's Spoon Bending Claims

In the 1970s, Uri Geller captivated audiences with his alleged psychic powers, famously bending spoons with his mind during televised performances. However, skeptics soon demonstrated that Geller's feats could be replicated using simple sleight of hand and misdirection, techniques commonly employed by magicians. Investigations by professional illusionists and scientific skeptics revealed that his spoon bending was not the result of supernatural abilities but rather clever tricks, challenging the authenticity of Geller's claims and sparking widespread debate about the nature of his performances.

The Learned English Dog

"The Learned English Dog," a performing border collie named Don, captivated audiences in London during the 19th century. He was famous for his ability to seemingly understand and respond to English commands. Don's owner, a night watchman named Thomas Burt, claimed that the dog could understand several languages and respond accordingly. Audiences were amazed as Don reportedly answered questions by barking the correct number of times to indicate numerical answers. This unique act drew considerable attention and was often highlighted in newspapers of the time, showcasing Victorian England's fascination with animal intelligence and the era's penchant for novelty entertainment acts. Don's performances blurred the line between genuine animal cognition and clever stage trickery, contributing to ongoing debates about the extent of animal understanding and communication.

The Howard Hughes Autobiography

The Howard Hughes autobiography hoax is a notorious literary fraud from the early 1970s. Clifford Irving, an American writer, claimed to have collaborated directly with the reclusive billionaire Howard Hughes on his autobiography, securing a lucrative deal with McGraw-Hill. Irving produced fake letters and notes to convince the publishers and even set up elaborate schemes to mimic Hughes' reclusiveness, which added credibility to his claims. The hoax was exposed when Hughes, who had been living in seclusion for years, broke his silence and denied any involvement in the project during a famously rare teleconference. This led to a legal investigation, and Irving was eventually convicted of fraud, serving time in prison. The incident remains one of the most audacious and talked-about literary hoaxes in publishing history.

Chapter Eight

Remarkable Recovery Stories

Aron Ralston: The Canyon Survivor

Aron Ralston's harrowing experience of survival captured worldwide attention in 2003 when he was forced to amputate his own right forearm with a dull multi-tool. This drastic measure came after his arm became trapped by a dislodged boulder during a solo canyoneering trip in Blue John Canyon, Utah. Ralston had not informed anyone of his hiking plans, leaving him without hope of rescue. After five days of entrapment, he realized that his survival depended on self-amputation. Following the amputation, he still had to rappel down a 65-foot cliff and hike several miles before he encountered other hikers who assisted him. Ralston's story of survival and resilience became the subject of the bestselling autobiography "Between a Rock and a Hard Place" and the Oscar-nominated film "127 Hours," directed by Danny Boyle and starring James Franco.

Bethany Hamilton: Surfing Beyond the Shark Attack

Bethany Hamilton became an inspiration worldwide after she survived a shark attack in 2003 while surfing off Kauai's North Shore, which resulted in the loss of her left arm. Despite this life-changing event, Hamilton returned to professional surfing just one month after the attack. Her incredible determination and skill not only allowed her to compete but also to win a national title in 2005. Bethany's story of overcoming adversity resonated globally, leading to the release of her autobiography, "Soul Surfer," which later inspired a 2011 biographical film of the same name. Hamilton continues to surf competitively and uses her platform to inspire others with her courage and unyielding faith.

The Chilean Miners: Buried Alive and Rescued

In 2010, the world watched in rapt attention as a dramatic rescue unfolded in Chile, where 33 miners were trapped 700 meters underground at the San José mine near Copiapó. After a cave-in blocked their exit, the miners were feared dead until they managed to attach a note to a drill bit that had pierced their refuge 17 days later, alerting rescuers that they were still alive. The miners survived 69 days underground before a meticulously planned rescue operation brought them safely to the surface. The rescue involved drilling a narrow escape shaft and lifting each miner out in a specially designed capsule, a feat of engineering and human endurance that captivated global audiences. This event not only showcased remarkable survival skills but also the power of international cooperation and human resilience.

Malala Yousafzai: From Tragedy to Triumph

Malala Yousafzai, a Pakistani activist for female education, became a global symbol of resilience and the struggle for women's rights after surviving an assassination attempt by the Taliban in 2012. Targeted for her outspoken advocacy for girls' education in her hometown of Swat Valley, Malala was shot in the head while on a school bus. Her miraculous recovery and unyielding dedication to her cause propelled her onto the world stage. In 2014, at just 17 years old, Malala became the youngest-ever recipient of the Nobel Peace Prize, recognized for her courageous and relentless advocacy for education under the most daunting and dangerous circumstances. Her story has inspired a worldwide movement for educational rights and has made her a prominent voice in global discussions on human rights and education.

Juliane Koepcke: The Sole Survivor of a Plane Crash

Juliane Koepcke's survival story is extraordinary and almost unbelievable. On Christmas Eve in 1971, at the age of 17, she was the sole survivor of LANSA Flight 508, a plane that disintegrated mid-air over the Peruvian rainforest due to a lightning strike. Remarkably, Koepcke survived a two-mile fall while still strapped to her seat, landing in the dense jungle canopy. Despite sustaining serious injuries, she managed to survive for 11 days alone in the rainforest. Using skills learned from her father, a biologist, and her own remarkable resilience, she navigated through the dense undergrowth and dangerous wildlife, eventually finding a small creek which led her to a local lumber camp. Her discovery and subsequent rescue became an incredible tale of human survival and endurance.

Nando Parrado: The Andes Mountain Miracle

Nando Parrado, one of the 16 survivors of the infamous 1972 Andes plane crash, is a testament to human resilience and heroism. After enduring 72 harrowing days in the brutal cold and isolation following the crash of Uruguayan Air Force Flight 571, which carried his rugby team and family members, Parrado played a crucial role in their survival. Facing extreme conditions, he and fellow survivor Roberto Canessa embarked on a grueling 10-day trek across the Andes Mountains without gear or proper nourishment. This extraordinary journey led them to find help, ultimately saving those who remained at the crash site. Parrado's story, one of the most remarkable survival stories ever recorded, highlights the incredible limits of human endurance and the power of unwavering determination.

Louis Zamperini: Unbroken Will

Louis Zamperini's life story is one of extraordinary resilience and redemption. An Olympic runner who competed in the 1936 Berlin Olympics, Zamperini's athletic career was interrupted by World War II, during which he served as a bombardier. In 1943, his aircraft was shot down over the Pacific, leading to a harrowing 47 days adrift on a life raft, facing starvation, dehydration, and shark attacks. His ordeal didn't end upon rescue; he was captured by Japanese forces and endured brutal treatment as a prisoner of war until the end of the conflict. Zamperini's unbroken spirit saw him through unimaginable challenges, and his post-war life, as detailed in Laura Hillenbrand's bestselling biography

"Unbroken," saw him forgive his captors and become an inspirational speaker, sharing his journey of survival, resilience, and forgiveness.

The Thai Cave Rescue: A Race Against Time

The Thai Cave Rescue in 2018 was a dramatic global effort that involved saving a group of 12 boys and their soccer coach who were trapped in the Tham Luang cave complex in northern Thailand. What makes this rescue particularly remarkable was the use of a full-face mask sedation technique, which was crucial for safely extracting the boys through the flooded and narrow cave passages. This method was proposed and implemented by Australian anesthetist Richard Harris, who was also an experienced cave diver. The sedation allowed the boys, most of whom couldn't swim, to remain calm and passive while divers navigated the complex and perilous routes to bring them to safety. This innovative approach was a key factor in the successful rescue, which involved over 100 divers and support from various countries, showcasing extraordinary international cooperation and human ingenuity under pressure.

Hugh Herr: Advancing Prosthetics After Tragedy

Hugh Herr is a pioneering figure in the field of biomechatronics, using his personal tragedy as a catalyst for innovation. After losing both of his legs below the knee due to severe frostbite during a climbing expedition in 1982, Herr turned his focus toward improving prosthetic technology. He is now the director of the Biomechatronics group at MIT's Media Lab, where he and his team develop advanced prosthetic limbs that offer increased mobility and new levels of functionality. Herr's work not only advances technology but also embodies his personal mission to eliminate disability through technological innovation. His groundbreaking contributions have resulted in sophisticated bionic devices that merge body and machine, significantly enhancing the lives of amputees worldwide.

Jessica Cox: Flying with Feet

Jessica Cox is renowned for being the world's first licensed armless pilot, a remarkable achievement that showcases the incredible potential of human adaptability and perseverance. Born without arms due to a rare birth defect, Cox has never allowed her physical condition to limit her aspirations or achievements. She controls the airplane using her feet, manipulating the controls with her toes. Cox's ability extends beyond flying; she is also a black belt in taekwondo, a motivational speaker, and an advocate for people with disabilities. Her extraordinary life challenges conventional perceptions of disability and demonstrates how determination and innovation can overcome formidable obstacles. Cox's achievements serve as a powerful example that challenges are not barriers, but invitations to reach new heights.

Terry Fox: A Marathon of Hope

Terry Fox is a Canadian hero best known for his Marathon of Hope, an ambitious cross-country run to raise money and awareness for cancer research. In 1980, despite having lost his right leg to osteosarcoma, Fox attempted to run across Canada, starting from St. John's, Newfoundland. Using a prosthetic leg, he ran the equivalent of a full marathon every day for 143 days, covering over 5,300 kilometers (3,300 miles) before the spread of his cancer forced him to stop near Thunder Bay, Ontario. His determination and selflessness have had a lasting impact; the Terry Fox Foundation has raised over $800 million for cancer research, making it one of the most successful fundraising events worldwide. Terry Fox's legacy lives on as millions participate in annual Terry Fox Runs held in over 25 countries.

Phineas Gage: The Man with a Rod Through His Head

Phineas Gage, a 19th-century railroad construction foreman, became one of the most famous cases in medical history following a dramatic accident in 1848 where a large iron rod was driven completely through his skull. Remarkably, Gage survived the incident, but his personality reportedly changed significantly, providing one of the first links between brain injury and personality change. This incident occurred when Gage was compacting explosive powder with a tamping iron, and a spark ignited the powder, causing the iron to shoot through his cheek, pass behind his eye socket, and exit through the top of his head. Gage's survival and subsequent behavioral changes were extensively studied and contributed to the early understanding of the brain's role in dictating personality, fundamentally altering the field of neurology and psychology.

The Miracle on the Hudson: Captain Sully's Heroic Landing

The "Miracle on the Hudson" refers to the emergency water landing of US Airways Flight 1549 on January 15, 2009, expertly executed by Captain Chesley "Sully" Sullenberger. Shortly after takeoff from New York City's LaGuardia Airport, the aircraft struck a flock of geese, which disabled both engines at a low altitude. With no power and limited options, Captain Sully and his co-pilot, Jeffrey Skiles, made the decision to ditch the plane in the Hudson River. Remarkably, all 155 people on board survived, thanks to the swift and calm actions of the crew, coordination with air traffic control, and immediate response from nearby ferry operators and emergency services. This incident not only highlighted the importance of pilot experience and training in aviation safety but also demonstrated extraordinary teamwork and professionalism under pressure.

Beck Weathers: Surviving the 1996 Everest Disaster

Beck Weathers' survival during the 1996 Mount Everest disaster is one of the most remarkable stories of human endurance and resilience. Weathers was part of an expedition that encountered a brutal blizzard while attempting to descend from the summit, which claimed eight lives. Stricken with severe hypothermia and left for dead, Weathers miraculously regained consciousness alone in the storm. Despite being severely frostbitten and virtually blind due to his impaired vision from a previous radial keratotomy, he managed to walk back to the camp. His survival required multiple complex surgeries to treat his frostbite, especially his hands, but he lived to tell his harrowing story. Weathers' ordeal and improbable survival were later featured in various books and films, including Jon Krakauer's "Into Thin Air" and the film "Everest," highlighting the perilous allure and deadly challenges of high-altitude mountaineering.

Jaycee Dugard: A Life Reclaimed

Jaycee Dugard's story is a profound example of resilience and recovery. Kidnapped at age 11 in 1991 while walking to a school bus stop in South Lake Tahoe, California, Dugard was held captive for 18 years in a concealed backyard compound by Phillip and Nancy Garrido. During this time, she was subjected to repeated abuse and bore two daughters fathered by her captor. Her discovery and rescue in 2009 came about when a campus police officer at the University of California, Berkeley, sensed something amiss during a meeting with Phillip Garrido and took the initiative to investigate further. Following her rescue, Jaycee has worked to reclaim her life, focusing on healing and advocating for families of missing persons. Her memoir, *A Stolen Life*, which chronicles her years in captivity and her journey towards healing, has inspired many with its message of hope and enduring strength in the face of unimaginable adversity.

Lone Survivor: Marcus Luttrell's Harrowing Tale

Marcus Luttrell's experience during Operation Red Wings in Afghanistan in 2005 is not only a testament to his survival but also to the unexpected kindness amidst war. After his SEAL team was compromised and ambushed, resulting in the deaths of his comrades, Luttrell was left severely injured. His survival became dependent on the local Pashtun villagers of Sabray, who invoked their cultural code of honor, Pashtunwali, which demands protection of those who seek asylum. Despite the risk of Taliban retaliation, the villagers provided medical care and safeguarded Luttrell until they could alert U.S. forces. This act of bravery and compassion highlights a profound intersection of cultural honor and humanity in the midst of conflict, providing a deeper layer to Lutrell's harrowing narrative.

Hiroo Onoda: The Last Japanese Soldier to Surrender

Hiroo Onoda was a Japanese intelligence officer who became famous for continuing to fight World War II until 1974, nearly three decades after the conflict had ended. Stationed on Lubang Island in the Philippines, Onoda was ordered not to surrender, a command he took to heart. He continued his guerrilla activities, surviving in the jungle, until he was officially relieved of duty by his former commanding officer who flew to the Philippines to formally rescind his orders. Onoda's incredible story is a poignant example of unwavering dedication and loyalty to orders, highlighting the psychological and physical extremes of wartime survival. His return to Japan was met with great public interest and he later moved to Brazil to become a cattle farmer before eventually returning to Japan to run a nature camp for kids, promoting survival skills.

The Apollo 13 Mission: A Successful Failure

The Apollo 13 mission, famously described as a "successful failure," demonstrated remarkable human ingenuity and the resilience of the human spirit under pressure. Launched on April 11, 1970, the mission suffered a catastrophic service module oxygen tank explosion two days later, which jeopardized the lives of astronauts Jim Lovell, Jack Swigert, and Fred Haise. Despite severe hardships caused by limited power, loss of cabin heat, and a shortage of potable water, the crew, along with mission control, ingeniously modified the lunar module into a lifeboat. This critical adjustment allowed them to safely navigate around the moon and return to Earth. Apollo 13's safe return transformed the mission into a profound lesson on crisis management and effective teamwork, underlining NASA's ability to solve complex problems in real-time.

Tami Oldham Ashcraft: Adrift at Sea

Tami Oldham Ashcraft's survival story is a gripping tale of resilience and determination. In 1983, while sailing from Tahiti to San Diego with her fiancé, Richard Sharp, their yacht was caught in a Category 4 hurricane. Ashcraft was knocked unconscious, and upon waking 27 hours later, she found herself alone, with Richard gone and the yacht severely damaged. Using only a sextant and watch to navigate, Ashcraft managed to sail the crippled yacht 1,500 miles to Hilo, Hawaii, over the course of 41 days. Despite suffering from severe injuries and exhaustion, her deep knowledge of sailing and unyielding willpower kept her going. Ashcraft's extraordinary journey of survival at sea is a testament to human endurance and has been the subject of books and the 2018 film adaptation, "Adrift."

Ricky Megee: Lost in the Outback

In 2006, Ricky Megee became a remarkable tale of survival after he was found by a group of farmworkers in the Australian Outback, where he had been lost for 71 days. His ordeal began when his car broke down in the remote wilderness, and under mysterious circumstances, he claimed he was drugged and left for dead. Megee survived by eating frogs, snakes, and lizards, and by collecting rainwater in an improvised dam he constructed. His drastic weight loss and the extreme conditions he endured showcased the harshness of the Outback and the human body's capacity to adapt in survival situations. Megee's story is not only a testament to human resilience but also highlights the dangers and unpredictability of Australia's vast interior.

The Andean Rugby Team: A Story of Endurance

The Andean rugby team's story of endurance and survival is one of the most compelling human dramas. In 1972, a plane carrying the Old Christians Club rugby team from Uruguay crashed into the Andes mountains. Stranded at a high altitude with minimal supplies and no hope of immediate rescue, the survivors endured brutal cold and life-threatening injuries. After 72 days isolated in the mountains, their plight worsened by an avalanche, they made the agonizing decision to survive by resorting to cannibalism of deceased passengers. Ultimately, two of the survivors embarked on a daring 10-day trek across the mountains to find help. Their successful return led to the rescue of the remaining 14 survivors. This profound story of survival against all odds was later recounted in the book "Alive" and adapted into a film, highlighting the depths of human resilience and the complex moral decisions faced in extreme situations.

Yossi Ghinsberg: Jungle Survivor

Yossi Ghinsberg's extraordinary survival story unfolded in 1981 when he was stranded in the Bolivian Amazon for three weeks. An Israeli adventurer, Ghinsberg traveled to Bolivia where he met three other travelers and ventured into the uncharted Amazon rainforest. However, their expedition went perilously wrong when Ghinsberg became separated from the group after a rafting accident on a river. Alone, without a knife, map, or survival training, he endured harrowing conditions, facing threats from wild animals, starvation, and the harsh elements of the jungle. Ghinsberg's ordeal ended when he was miraculously found by his friends who had organized a search party. His gripping tale of survival was later chronicled in his book "Jungle," which also inspired a major motion picture, highlighting his incredible resilience and the profound will to survive against all odds.

Steven Callahan: 76 Days Adrift

Steven Callahan's tale of survival is one of the most remarkable maritime stories. In 1982, while sailing alone across the Atlantic Ocean, his sailboat, the Napoleon Solo, was severely damaged by a storm, leaving him adrift on a five-and-a-half-foot life raft for 76 days. His ingenuity in the face of adversity was astounding; Callahan survived by catching fish and birds with spears he fashioned from the wreckage, and he collected drinking water from rain using a makeshift collection system. Despite multiple shark attacks and severe storms, he maintained his morale by keeping a daily log and navigating using the stars. His eventual rescue came after he had drifted more than 1,800 miles. Callahan's experience, documented in his book "Adrift: Seventy-six Days Lost at Sea," has since been a vital resource in survival literature and inspired aspects of the 2012 film "Life of Pi."

The Essex Whaleship Disaster: The Real Moby-Dick

The Essex whaleship disaster of 1820 is one of the most harrowing maritime tragedies in history and served as the real-life inspiration for Herman Melville's "Moby-Dick." The Essex was rammed and sunk by a sperm whale in the South Pacific, leaving its crew stranded in lifeboats thousands of miles from land. The survivors faced extreme hardships, resorting to cannibalism to stay alive. After more than 90 days at sea, only eight of the twenty crew members were rescued. The ordeal of the Essex was documented in the first mate Owen Chase's account, which became a key narrative source for Melville. This disaster not only influenced one of the greatest American novels but also underscored the perilous nature of the whaling industry and its impact on literature and history.

Mauro Prosperi: Lost in the Sahara

Mauro Prosperi, an Italian police officer and endurance athlete, faced an extraordinary survival challenge during the 1994 Marathon des Sables, a grueling 155-mile ultramarathon through the Sahara Desert. During a sandstorm, Prosperi lost his way, stranding him in one of the most inhospitable environments on Earth. Rather than succumbing to despair, he demonstrated remarkable resilience by surviving for ten days on his limited supplies. He drank his own urine and bat blood, and even trapped and ate lizards to sustain himself. Prosperi found shelter in an abandoned shrine and attempted to signal for help by writing "SOS" in the sand before finally being discovered by a nomadic family.

He had traveled over 180 miles off course. This harrowing experience cut short his race but amplified his legend as a survivor in extreme conditions.

Chris McCandless: Into the Wild

Chris McCandless, immortalized in Jon Krakauer's book "Into the Wild," ventured into the Alaskan wilderness in April 1992 seeking a life stripped of societal confines. After hitchhiking to Alaska and entering the wild with minimal supplies, McCandless survived for approximately 113 days in the remote backcountry, primarily residing in an abandoned bus known as "Fairbanks Bus 142." His adventure ended tragically when he likely died from starvation, exacerbated by possible poisoning from mistakenly eating toxic plants. McCandless's story, which explores themes of adventure, solitude, and the harsh realities of nature, continues to resonate deeply, sparking debates about the allure and dangers of wilderness exploration. His life and journey have been both celebrated and critiqued, symbolizing the eternal human quest for meaning and connection with nature.

The Robertson Family: Shipwrecked in the Pacific

In 1972, the Robertson family embarked on a sailing adventure that turned into a fight for survival when their yacht, the Lucette, was sunk by killer whales in the Pacific Ocean. Led by patriarch Dougal Robertson, the family of five, along with a friend, survived for 38 days adrift on a small life raft and an inflatable dinghy. Their survival hinged on their ingenuity and determination; they caught fish, turtles, and rainwater, and even devised a system to distill drinking water using makeshift stills. The ordeal tested their physical and mental limits but ultimately highlighted their resilience and resourcefulness. The Robertson family's extraordinary survival story has been documented in several books and remains a testament to human endurance and the will to survive against all odds.

Jose Salvador Alvarenga: The Castaway Fisherman

Jose Salvador Alvarenga's survival story is one of the most extraordinary human endurance tales of modern times. In November 2012, Alvarenga, a Salvadoran fisherman, set out on a routine fishing trip from Mexico, only to be caught in a severe storm that set him adrift in the Pacific Ocean. Remarkably, he survived for 438 days lost at sea, living off fish, birds, and turtles that he caught with his hands, and drinking rainwater and occasionally turtle blood for hydration. His small fishing boat drifted over 6,700 miles from the coast of Mexico to the Marshall Islands, where he eventually washed ashore in January 2014. Alvarenga's almost unbelievable saga of survival showcases the extremes of human resilience and the will to live, even in the most desperate conditions.

Shackleton's Endurance Expedition: Antarctic Survival

Shackleton's Endurance Expedition of 1914-1916 is one of the most remarkable survival stories in the history of exploration. Sir Ernest Shackleton and his crew set out to cross Antarctica via the South Pole but never reached the continent. Their ship, the Endurance, was trapped and eventually crushed by pack ice in the Weddell Sea, stranding the men on the ice. Remarkably, all 28 crew members survived. Shackleton and five others then made an 800-mile open boat journey in the lifeboat *James Caird* to South Georgia, from where they organized a rescue for the rest of the crew. This expedition is famed not just for its incredible hardships, but for Shackleton's leadership, under which not a single crew member's life was lost. The saga stands as a testament to human endurance, resourcefulness, and the power of effective leadership in the face of overwhelming odds.

Norman Ollestad: Boy Wonder of the San Gabriels

Norman Ollestad's gripping tale of survival and resilience is chronicled in his memoir, "Crazy for the Storm." At the age of 11, he was the sole survivor of a tragic plane crash that occurred in the San Gabriel Mountains in 1979. The plane, carrying Norman, his father, his father's girlfriend, and the pilot, crashed into the mountains during a snowstorm. Norman's survival skills were largely attributed to the demanding physical training and extreme sports his father encouraged him to undertake from a very young age. After the crash, using the skills he learned from his father, Norman managed to navigate down the treacherous, icy mountain to safety, enduring severe weather conditions and physical injuries. His story is not only a harrowing account of survival against the odds but also a touching narrative about the profound influence his father had on his life.

Tommy McHugh: A Second Chance to Become an Artist

Tommy McHugh's life took an extraordinary turn after he suffered a near-fatal brain hemorrhage at the age of 51, which led to a sudden and profound burst of artistic and poetic expression, a phenomenon sometimes referred to as "Acquired Savant Syndrome." Before the incident, McHugh had no notable interest or skill in art or poetry. However, post-recovery, he found himself compelled to create, producing thousands of paintings, sculptures, and poems. His case has fascinated neuroscientists and psychologists, as it raises intriguing questions about the hidden capacities of the brain and the transformative potential of neuroplasticity. McHugh's story is not just about surviving a medical emergency but also about the unexpected gifts that such profound experiences can unlock, dramatically altering the trajectory of a person's life.

Douglas Mawson: Alone in Antarctica

Douglas Mawson, an Australian polar explorer and geologist, faced extreme survival challenges during the Australasian Antarctic Expedition of 1911-1914. After his two companions died, Mawson continued alone, navigating through some of the most inhospitable conditions on Earth. What makes his journey particularly harrowing is the fact that, on his solitary trek back to base camp, he fell through a snow-covered crevasse, but miraculously saved himself by catching the sledge harness, which wedged in the ice above him. Despite suffering from starvation, hypothermia, and severe physical deterioration, Mawson traveled over 100 miles alone, eventually making it back to base camp—just hours after a rescue ship had departed. He had to wait nearly another year for rescue. Mawson's ordeal is one of the greatest survival stories in the annals of Antarctic exploration, demonstrating incredible human endurance against all odds.

Harrison Okene: The Man Who Survived Underwater

Harrison Okene's survival story is one of incredible endurance under the most extreme conditions. In 2013, while working as a cook on the tugboat Jacson-4, the vessel capsized and sank to the bottom of the Atlantic Ocean off the Nigerian coast due to heavy swells. Okene found himself trapped in a four-foot high air pocket under 30 meters (about 100 feet) of freezing water, dressed only in his boxer shorts. Remarkably, he survived for nearly three days in this pitch-dark, cold environment by sipping from a can of Coke and finding a mattress to stay afloat, all while breathing an ever-decreasing supply of oxygen. Divers, initially dispatched to recover bodies, were astonished to find Okene alive, making his rescue an extraordinary feat. His dramatic survival, often referred to as the "Nigerian Miracle," underscores the profound will to live and the body's capacity to endure against seemingly insurmountable odds.

Joe Simpson: Touching the Void

Joe Simpson's survival story, famously recounted in his book "Touching the Void," is a testament to human resilience. In 1985, while descending from the summit of Siula Grande in the Peruvian Andes, Simpson suffered a severe leg break. Believing him to be mortally injured, his climbing partner, Simon Yates, attempted to lower him to safety. However, Simpson ended up dangling over a precipice, forcing Yates to make the harrowing decision to cut the rope to avoid being pulled down himself. Simpson fell approximately 150 feet into a crevasse but miraculously survived. Despite his injuries and severe frostbite, he managed to crawl and hop five miles back to their base camp, a journey that took three agonizing days. Simpson's ordeal has become one of the most famous mountaineering survival stories ever recorded, highlighting extreme perseverance and the drive to survive against all odds.

Ann Rodgers: Lost in the Arizona Wilderness

In 2016, Ann Rodgers, a 72-year-old woman, survived nine days lost in the vast wilderness of the White Mountains of Arizona after her hybrid vehicle ran out of gas and electricity. Stranded in a remote area, Rodgers, along with her dog and cat, ventured into the rugged terrain in search of help and signal coverage. To sustain herself, she drank pond water and ate plants and berries she identified using her survival knowledge. She also spelled out "HELP" on the ground with sticks and rocks, which was eventually spotted by a search helicopter. Her experience showcases not only the critical importance of wilderness survival skills but also the human capacity to adapt and persevere in the face of extreme challenges.

Rosie Swale-Pope: Running Around the World

Rosie Swale-Pope is a remarkable adventurer known for her solo circumnavigation of the globe on foot, a feat that took her five years to complete, from 2003 to 2008. At the age of 57, she embarked on this journey, running over 20,000 miles across multiple continents, facing extreme weather, wild animals, and challenging terrains. Swale-Pope undertook this extraordinary endeavor to raise awareness and funds for cancer research, inspired by the loss of her husband to the disease. Her adventure included traversing Russia during one of its coldest winters, where temperatures plunged to minus 62 degrees Celsius, showcasing her incredible endurance and commitment to her cause. Rosie's journey is not just a testament to human endurance but also a profound statement on the power of human spirit and purpose.

Peter Skyllberg: Surviving the Swedish Winter

In 2012, Peter Skyllberg survived an extraordinary ordeal when he was trapped in his car under snow for two months during a harsh Swedish winter near Umeå. The temperatures outside dipped below -30 degrees Celsius (-22 degrees Fahrenheit), yet Skyllberg managed to stay alive in the insulated environment of his car, which essentially became an improvised snow cave. Remarkably, he survived by eating only snow to stay hydrated, entering a state akin to hibernation, which significantly slowed down his metabolism and reduced his nutritional needs. Rescuers discovered him in what seemed to be a weak but stable condition, astonished to find someone alive after such an extended period in such extreme conditions. Skyllberg's survival is often cited as a medical anomaly and a testament to the human body's extraordinary capacity to adapt to severe cold.

Ada Blackjack: The Lone Survivor of Wrangel Island

Ada Blackjack, an Iñupiat woman, emerged as a remarkable survivor of a tragic Arctic expedition to Wrangel Island in 1921. Originally joining the team as a seamstress and cook, Blackjack found herself the sole survivor after the expedition faced harsh conditions and dwindling supplies, leading to the deaths of all other team members. Over two years, she endured the brutal Arctic environment, teaching herself survival skills such as hunting and trapping to fend for herself and her ill companion before he too succumbed. Blackjack was eventually rescued in 1923. Her incredible story of survival made her a reluctant heroine; she was initially hired for her sewing skills but proved to be an adept survivor, utilizing her intelligence and adaptability to outlive her male counterparts and return to civilization.

The Dionne Quintuplets: Surviving Fame

The Dionne Quintuplets, born in 1934 in Ontario, Canada, were the first quintuplets known to have survived their infancy. The immense public interest they generated led the Canadian government to take them under its wardship for the first nine years of their lives, during which time they were displayed to the public in a theme park-like setting called "Quintland." This attraction drew over three million visitors by 1943, making it more popular than Niagara Falls during that period.

Luis Urzua: The Last Miner Out

Luis Urzua, the shift foreman during the 2010 Chilean mining disaster, was instrumental in leading and organizing 33 miners trapped 700 meters underground. Demonstrating remarkable leadership, he was the last to be rescued after 69 days, ensuring all his men were safely extracted before him. His strict rationing of food and his ability to map their underground location were crucial for their survival and the success of the rescue mission.

Daniel Kish: The Real Batman

Daniel Kish, who lost his sight to retinal cancer before his first birthday, is renowned for his extraordinary ability to navigate the world using echolocation. By clicking his tongue and listening to the echoes, Kish can identify the location and texture of objects in his environment, a technique similar to that used by bats. His proficiency in this unique skill has earned him the nickname "the real-life Batman." He has also founded World Access for the Blind, an organization that teaches echolocation to visually impaired individuals, empowering them to achieve greater independence.

Alcides Moreno's Miraculous Survival and Recovery

In 2007, Alcides Moreno, a window washer in New York City, survived an astonishing 47-story fall from a skyscraper. Despite sustaining severe injuries, including multiple fractures and internal damage, Moreno's resilience and determination led to a miraculous recovery. Defying all odds, he was able to walk again within a year, showcasing an incredible example of human survival and the effectiveness of modern medical treatment. His story continues to inspire many, highlighting the potential for recovery even in the face of seemingly insurmountable challenges.

Winston Churchill's Daring Escape and Journey to Freedom

As a young officer during the Second Boer War, Winston Churchill was captured and imprisoned in a POW camp in South Africa. Demonstrating remarkable courage and resourcefulness, he managed to escape from the camp and embarked on a perilous 300-mile journey to safety. His daring escape not only showcased his indomitable spirit but also garnered him significant attention and acclaim, boosting his political career. This extraordinary feat contributed to his reputation for resilience and tenacity, qualities that would later define his leadership during World War II.

Frane Selak: The World's Luckiest Man

Frane Selak, often referred to as "the world's luckiest man," is known for his incredible series of escapes from deadly situations. Over the course of his life, the Croatian music teacher survived a train derailment, a door-less flight accident, a bus crash, two car fires, and a car accident where his vehicle plunged into a river. Remarkably, after surviving these harrowing incidents, Selak won the lottery in 2003, cementing his reputation for having an almost mythical level of good fortune.

Truman Duncan: The Half-Man

Truman Duncan miraculously survived a severe accident in 2006, where he was run over by a train, severing his lower body. Despite losing both legs and suffering multiple internal injuries, Duncan remained conscious during the ordeal and astoundingly phoned emergency services himself. After undergoing multiple surgeries and enduring a grueling recovery process, he returned to work at the railyard. Duncan's extraordinary resilience and determination to overcome his physical limitations have made his story one of remarkable survival and adaptability.

Lincoln Hall: Left for Dead on Everest

Lincoln Hall is famously known for his miraculous survival on Mount Everest in 2006. After reaching the summit, Hall suffered from cerebral edema during his descent and was left for dead by his climbing team just below the summit. Astonishingly, he was found alive the next day by another climbing group, sitting cross-legged on the mountain's edge. His survival after spending a night exposed at such an altitude without oxygen or proper equipment is one of the most extraordinary incidents in the history of Everest expeditions.

Amy Purdy: Defying Limits on the Dance Floor

Amy Purdy, a double amputee and Paralympic snowboarder, defied expectations by competing on the popular TV show "Dancing with the Stars." After losing her legs below the knee to bacterial meningitis at 19, Purdy pursued an athletic career, later showcasing her remarkable adaptability and spirit on the dance floor. Partnered with professional dancer Derek Hough, she finished as a runner-up in the 18th season, inspiring many with her fluid dance moves and the innovative use of her prosthetic legs in her performances.

Xia Boyu: Conquering Everest with Prosthetic Legs

Xia Boyu, a Chinese climber, made headlines when he successfully summited Mount Everest in 2018 at the age of 69, despite having both of his legs amputated below the knee. His ascent was especially remarkable as it was his fifth attempt; his first was in 1975 when he lost his legs due to frostbite after giving his sleeping bag to a teammate in distress. Xia's story is not only one of personal triumph over physical limitations but also highlights advancements in prosthetic technology that enabled him to conquer one of the most challenging peaks in the world.

James Braddock's Inspirational Comeback in the Great Depression

James Braddock, known as "Cinderella Man," exemplified resilience by overcoming poverty and injury during the Great Depression to win the heavyweight championship in 1935. His career had nearly ended due to a string of losses and injuries, forcing him to work as a laborer to support his family. However, Braddock made a remarkable comeback, culminating in his victory against Max Baer, the reigning champion. His underdog story and triumph against overwhelming odds inspired the 2005 film "Cinderella Man," highlighting his perseverance and the hope he provided during a challenging era.

Edgar Harrell: Surviving the USS Indianapolis

Edgar Harrell was a survivor of the USS Indianapolis, a U.S. Navy ship that was tragically sunk by a Japanese submarine in 1945 after delivering parts of the atomic bomb that would be dropped on Hiroshima. The sinking led to one of the worst naval disasters in American history due to the delayed rescue operation, leaving survivors in shark-infested waters for four days. Harrell, among the few who survived, later recounted his harrowing experience in public speeches and a book, providing a personal account of the survival instinct, camaraderie, and faith that kept him alive during those critical days.

Chapter Nine

Extraordinary Exploits of Everyday Items

The Paperclip: A Symbol of Resistance

During World War II, the paperclip emerged as a symbol of resistance in Norway against Nazi occupation. Norwegians quietly clipped paperclips to their clothing as a covert sign of solidarity and unity against the occupiers. The seemingly mundane object was chosen because it represented binding together and was a subtle way of showing resistance without drawing the severe punishments associated with more overt acts of defiance. This small act of rebellion became a powerful symbol of resistance and national pride during a time of intense oppression.

Bubble Wrap: Intended as Wallpaper

Bubble wrap, the ubiquitous packing material known for its protective bubbles, was originally invented in 1957 with the intention of being used as textured wallpaper. Engineers Alfred Fielding and Marc Chavannes sealed two shower curtains together, trapping air bubbles between them with the hope of selling it as a trendy, easy-to-clean wallpaper. When the product failed to catch on in the home decor market, they discovered its efficacy in packaging, leading to its widespread adoption for protecting fragile items during shipping. Today, bubble wrap is celebrated not only for its practical uses but also for the simple joy of popping its bubbles.

Tea Bags: An Accidental Invention

Tea bags were an accidental invention by New York tea merchant Thomas Sullivan in the early 20th century. Initially, Sullivan sent samples of tea leaves to his customers in small, silk bags as a cost-effective way to distribute portions. His customers, misunderstanding the intended use, steeped the entire bag in hot water, finding the method convenient and effective. Pleased with the unexpected ease of use, they requested more of these novel "tea bags." Sullivan then crafted the idea into a product, switching from silk to gauze, and later to paper, which revolutionized the way people brewed their tea.

Post-it Notes: A Failed Adhesive Experiment

Post-it Notes originated from a failed attempt to create a strong adhesive in the laboratories of 3M in 1968. Scientist Spencer Silver developed a pressure-sensitive adhesive, but it was considered a failure because it was too weak for industrial applications—it could easily be peeled off without leaving any residue. However, in a twist of fate, a colleague, Art Fry, realized the potential of this adhesive for a bookmark that wouldn't slip out of his hymnal during choir practice. This insight led to the development of repositionable notes, which became commercially available in 1980 and soon turned into an essential tool for communication and organization worldwide.

The Frisbee: Inspired by Pie Tins

The Frisbee, a popular flying disc toy, was inspired by pie tins from the Frisbie Pie Company in Connecticut. In the 1940s, Yale University students discovered that empty pie tins from the company could be tossed and caught for entertainment. They would shout "Frisbie!" to warn each other of the incoming tin, mimicking the company's name stamped on each pie container. Building on this spontaneous game, Walter Morrison invented a plastic version of the disc, which was later marketed by Wham-O as the "Frisbee" in 1957, transforming a simple pastime into a worldwide recreational phenomenon.

Potatoes: The First Vegetable Grown in Space

Potatoes hold the distinction of being the first vegetable grown in space. In 1995, as part of a collaborative project between NASA and the University of Wisconsin, potato plants were successfully cultivated aboard the Space Shuttle Columbia during the STS-73 mission. This experiment aimed to explore the possibilities of supporting life in outer space through food production, using a special growth chamber called the Bioregenerative Planetary Life Support Systems Test Complex. The successful cultivation of potatoes in a microgravity environment marked a significant milestone in the research of sustainable life support systems for long-duration space missions.

The Slinky: A Naval Equipment Misstep

The Slinky, a popular coiled toy, was originally developed from a torsion spring designed to stabilize sensitive naval equipment on ships during World War II. Inventor Richard James, a mechanical engineer, noticed that one of his springs, when accidentally knocked off a shelf, continued to move gracefully across the floor. Intrigued by the spring's unique motion, James and his wife Betty saw its potential as a toy. In 1945, they demonstrated the Slinky at a department store in Philadelphia, where it became an instant hit, selling its entire inventory of 400 units in just ninety minutes, thus beginning its journey as a classic toy beloved by generations.

Microwave Ovens: Born from Radar Technology

Microwave ovens, now a commonplace kitchen appliance, were born out of radar technology developed during World War II. Percy Spencer, an engineer working on radar technology at Raytheon, accidentally discovered the cooking properties of microwave radiation when a candy bar melted in his pocket while he was standing near a radar set. Intrigued by this incident, Spencer conducted further experiments, including one where he successfully cooked popcorn with microwaves and another where an egg exploded. These experiments led to the development of the first commercial microwave oven in 1947, initially called the "Radarange."

The Safety Pin: A Hasty Invention for Debt

The safety pin was invented in 1849 by Walter Hunt, an American mechanic, as a quick solution to settle a $15 debt. Hunt devised the safety pin in just three hours, incorporating a spring mechanism and a clasp shield, which were innovative features that prevented the pin from opening unexpectedly and provided safety to the user. Realizing the practical utility of his creation, Hunt patented the safety pin and sold the rights for $400, using the proceeds to pay off his debt. This invention quickly became an essential item in everyday life, demonstrating a remarkable blend of simplicity and utility.

Coca-Cola: Originally a Medicinal Elixir

Coca-Cola was originally concocted as a medicinal elixir by John Pemberton, a pharmacist, in 1886 in Atlanta, Georgia. Seeking a remedy for his own ailments and hoping to capitalize on the growing demand for health tonics, Pemberton created a syrup that he marketed as a cure for various common ailments, including morphine addiction, indigestion, nerve disorders, and headaches. The original formula contained extracts of cocaine from the coca leaf and caffeine-rich kola nuts, which is how the beverage derived its name. It was first sold at Jacob's Pharmacy in Atlanta as a soda fountain drink, promoting it as a valuable brain tonic and intellectual beverage.

Velcro: Inspired by Burdock Burrs

Velcro, the widely used hook-and-loop fastener, was invented by Swiss engineer George de Mestral in 1941, inspired by a nature walk with his dog. De Mestral noticed that burdock burrs clung tenaciously to his clothing and his dog's fur. Upon examining the burrs under a microscope, he observed the tiny hooks that latched onto the loops in fabric and fur. This natural mechanism inspired him to create a synthetic fastening system that mimicked the burrs' gripping properties. After years of development and refinement, Velcro was patented in 1955 and has since become a staple fastening solution in various industries, from fashion to aerospace.

Lipstick: A Marker of Social Status

Lipstick has long been a marker of social status and power, dating back to ancient civilizations. In ancient Egypt, both men and women adorned their lips with crushed gemstones and minerals, not only for aesthetic purposes but also to signify their social rank and ward off evil spirits. Cleopatra famously used a blend of crushed carmine beetles and ants to create her signature red shade. Similarly, in ancient Greece, lipstick was used by courtesans to signify their profession, and laws even required them to wear it to avoid misleading potential clients. Over centuries, lipstick has evolved into a symbol of fashion and personal expression, maintaining its cultural significance across various societies.

The Pencil: A Graphite Discovery

The modern pencil traces its origins to a significant graphite discovery in the 16th century. In the early 1500s, a large deposit of pure, solid graphite was found in Borrowdale, England. Local shepherds initially used chunks of this soft mineral to mark their sheep, soon realizing its potential for writing and drawing. To make the material more manageable, the graphite was cut into sticks and wrapped in sheepskin or wood, creating the first crude pencils. This simple yet effective tool revolutionized writing and drawing, eventually leading to the mass-produced pencils we use today, encased in wood with a core of graphite mixed with clay for durability and varying hardness.

The QWERTY Keyboard: Designed to Prevent Jamming

The QWERTY keyboard layout, now ubiquitous on computers and typewriters, was originally designed in the 1870s by Christopher Latham Sholes to address a specific mechanical problem. Early typewriters had a tendency to jam when adjacent keys were pressed in quick succession. To mitigate this issue, Sholes arranged the keys in such a way that commonly used letter pairs were spaced farther apart, reducing the likelihood of jams. This seemingly counterintuitive design effectively slowed typists down just enough to prevent mechanical interference, leading to the widespread adoption of the QWERTY layout, which remains the standard despite advances in typing technology.

Sunglasses: Originating from Ancient Civilizations

Sunglasses, widely used today for fashion and eye protection, have their origins in ancient civilizations. The Inuit people created the earliest versions using flattened walrus ivory with narrow slits to protect their eyes from the harsh glare of sunlight reflecting off the snow. In ancient China, judges wore smoke-tinted quartz lenses to conceal their eye expressions during courtroom proceedings. By the 12th century, these rudimentary sunglasses had evolved, and their primary function was to reduce glare and improve vision in bright conditions, paving the way for the modern sunglasses we use today.

The Zipper: From Shoes to Fashion

The zipper, a ubiquitous fastening device, began its journey in the world of footwear. Invented by Whitcomb Judson in 1893, the initial design was intended as a "clasp locker" for shoes, aiming to simplify the process of fastening high-top boots. Despite its innovative concept, Judson's early zipper design was cumbersome and failed to gain commercial success. It wasn't until Swedish-American engineer Gideon Sundback improved the design in 1913, making it more reliable and easier to manufacture, that the zipper found widespread use. This enhanced version, initially marketed as the "hookless fastener," eventually revolutionized the fashion industry, becoming a staple in clothing, accessories, and countless everyday items.

Chewing Gum: An Ancient Practice

Chewing gum, a common treat today, has ancient origins that date back thousands of years. The earliest known chewers were the ancient Greeks, who enjoyed masticating a resin called mastiche derived from the mastic tree. Similarly, the Mayans and Aztecs chewed chicle, a latex sap from the sapodilla tree, for its enjoyable texture and to freshen breath. Native Americans also chewed resin from spruce trees, a practice observed by European settlers who later adopted it. These natural gums evolved into the commercial chewing gum industry in the 19th century when inventor Thomas Adams experimented with chicle, eventually creating the first modern chewing gum products.

The Umbrella: A Status Symbol

The umbrella, now a practical accessory for rain protection, once served as a significant status symbol. In ancient Egypt, umbrellas were used exclusively by nobility and religious leaders to shield themselves from the sun, symbolizing their elevated status and divine connection. These early parasols were often lavishly decorated with feathers and precious materials. Similarly, in ancient China, umbrellas marked the rank and social hierarchy, with only the emperor allowed to use yellow silk parasols. Over time, the umbrella's function expanded beyond sun protection, becoming a fashionable and practical tool for shielding against rain, yet its historical association with prestige and authority remains notable.

Kleenex: From Face Masks to Facial Tissue

Kleenex, the well-known brand of facial tissue, was initially developed for a very different purpose. During World War I, Kimberly-Clark Corporation created a crepe paper material called "Cellucotton" to be used in gas mask filters. After the war, with a surplus of this material, the company sought new uses and marketed it as a makeup remover. By the 1920s, Kleenex had been rebranded and advertised for its softness and convenience as a disposable handkerchief, leading to its widespread adoption for facial tissue. This innovative repurposing transformed it into an everyday household item.

Jeans: Durable Workwear

Jeans, now a global fashion staple, originated as durable workwear for laborers in the 19th century. Invented by Jacob Davis and Levi Strauss in 1873, the first jeans were designed to withstand the rigors of manual labor. Using sturdy denim fabric and reinforced with copper rivets at stress points, they were initially popular among miners, cowboys, and railroad workers. The practical design and rugged durability of jeans quickly earned them a reputation for reliability in harsh working conditions. Over time, they transitioned from functional workwear to a fashion icon, becoming a symbol of casual style and rebellion in the 20th century.

The Can Opener: A Post-Canned Food Invention

The can opener, a common kitchen tool, was actually invented decades after the invention of canned food. When canned food was first introduced in the early 19th century, it was sealed with heavy-duty soldering, making it difficult to open. Soldiers and consumers had to rely on knives, chisels, or even rocks to access the contents. It wasn't until 1858, nearly 50 years later, that Ezra Warner patented the first practical can opener, which featured a pointed blade and lever design. This innovation made it significantly easier and safer to open cans, transforming the way people accessed preserved food and contributing to the widespread adoption of canned goods.

High Heels: Originally for Men

High heels, now primarily associated with women's fashion, were originally designed for men. In the 16th century, Persian cavalrymen wore high-heeled shoes to secure their feet in stirrups, enhancing their stability and control while riding horses. This practical use of heels spread to Europe, where they became a symbol of power and status among the male aristocracy. Notably, King Louis XIV of France popularized high heels in the 17th century, often wearing elaborately decorated shoes with red heels to signify his royal privilege. It wasn't until the 18th century that high heels transitioned into women's fashion, becoming the stylish accessory we recognize today.

The Toothbrush: From Twigs to Bristles

The toothbrush, an essential tool for oral hygiene, has ancient origins that date back thousands of years. Early forms of toothbrushes were twigs called "chew sticks," used by ancient civilizations like the Egyptians and Babylonians around 3500 BCE. These sticks were frayed at one end to create a brush-like surface. The modern toothbrush design with bristles emerged in China during the Tang Dynasty (619-907 CE), using hog bristles attached to bamboo or bone handles. This design eventually made its way to Europe, where softer materials like horsehair were used. The first mass-produced toothbrush, resembling today's design, was created by William Addis in England in 1780, further evolving into the nylon-bristled versions we use today.

The Alarm Clock: A Plato Invention

The alarm clock's origins can be traced back to the ancient Greek philosopher Plato, who invented a water clock with an alarm signal around 400 BCE. This early device, known as a "clepsydra," used the flow of water to measure time. Plato's version was designed to alert his students to the start of his lectures at dawn. The clock worked by slowly filling a vessel with water; once it reached a certain level, it caused a whistle to sound, creating the first known instance of an alarm clock. This invention highlights Plato's ingenuity and the long history of humanity's efforts to manage and keep track of time.

The Jigsaw Puzzle: An Educational Tool

The jigsaw puzzle, now a popular pastime, was originally invented as an educational tool in the 1760s by John Spilsbury, a British mapmaker and engraver. Spilsbury created the first jigsaw puzzle by mounting a map on a sheet of hardwood and then cutting around the borders of each country. This innovative method allowed children to learn geography through an engaging and hands-on activity. The pieces had to be reassembled correctly to form the map, making it an effective learning aid. Over time, jigsaw puzzles evolved into various themes and complexities, becoming a beloved form of entertainment for all ages while maintaining their educational roots.

The Escalator: A Moving Staircase Concept

The escalator, a moving staircase concept, was first introduced to the public as an amusement ride rather than a practical means of transport. Invented by Jesse W. Reno in 1891, the earliest version was installed at Coney Island, New York, in 1896. This original "inclined elevator" was a novelty attraction, carrying passengers up a 25-degree incline on a conveyor belt with cleats. It wasn't until the early 20th century that the escalator was adapted for commercial use in department stores and public transit systems, revolutionizing the way people moved within buildings and enhancing urban mobility.

The Calculator: From Abacus to Digital

The calculator's evolution from the abacus to the digital age showcases centuries of innovation in computation. The abacus, developed around 500 BCE in ancient Mesopotamia, was the first known tool for arithmetic calculations, using beads slid on rods to represent numbers. Fast forward to the 17th century, and Blaise Pascal invented the Pascaline, an early mechanical calculator that could perform addition and subtraction. The 20th century saw the introduction of the electronic calculator, with significant advancements in the 1960s leading to pocket-sized versions. These digital calculators, powered by microchips, revolutionized mathematics by making complex calculations accessible to everyone, from students to professionals.

The Barcode: A Grocery Store Revolution

The barcode, a technology that revolutionized grocery stores, was inspired by Morse code. Invented by Norman Joseph Woodland and Bernard Silver in the late 1940s, the idea emerged when Woodland drew lines in the sand to mimic Morse code, envisioning a way to encode product information. The first commercial use of barcodes occurred on June 26, 1974, when a pack of Wrigley's Juicy Fruit gum was scanned at a Marsh Supermarket in Ohio. This simple yet transformative technology streamlined inventory management and checkout processes, forever changing the retail industry by increasing efficiency and accuracy in tracking products.

The Rubber Band: From Vulcanized Rubber

The rubber band, a staple of everyday life, owes its existence to the invention of vulcanized rubber. In 1845, British inventor Stephen Perry of the rubber manufacturing company Messers Perry and Co., London, patented the first rubber band, utilizing Charles Goodyear's process of vulcanization, which made rubber more durable and elastic. Perry's invention was initially designed to hold papers and envelopes together, providing a simple yet effective solution for organizing documents. This practical use quickly expanded, and rubber bands have since become indispensable in various applications, from industrial uses to household tasks, showcasing the versatility of vulcanized rubber.

The Shopping Cart: A Supermarket Innovation

The shopping cart, an essential tool in supermarkets today, was invented in 1937 by Sylvan Goldman, owner of the Humpty Dumpty supermarket chain in Oklahoma. Faced with the challenge of customers limiting their purchases due to the weight of handheld baskets, Goldman innovated a solution by attaching wheels to a folding chair, creating the first shopping cart. Initially, shoppers were reluctant to use the new invention, so Goldman hired models to push the carts around his store, demonstrating their convenience. This clever marketing tactic quickly caught on, and shopping carts soon became a ubiquitous feature in grocery stores, transforming the shopping experience by allowing customers to buy more items with ease.

The Light Bulb: Edison's Bright Idea

Thomas Edison is often credited with inventing the light bulb, but the invention was a culmination of efforts by several inventors over decades. Edison's significant contribution was improving the existing design to create a practical and long-lasting light bulb. In 1879, he developed a carbon filament that could burn for up to 1200 hours, a major advancement over previous designs that burned out quickly. Edison's team also devised an entire electrical lighting system, including generators and wiring, making widespread use of electric light possible. This breakthrough led to the widespread adoption of electric lighting, revolutionizing how people lived and worked after dark.

The Waffle Iron: A Culinary Staple

The waffle iron, now a beloved kitchen appliance, has roots dating back to the Middle Ages. The first waffle irons were made of cast iron and featured intricate patterns, often depicting religious symbols or family crests. These irons were designed to be held over an open flame, imprinting the unique designs onto the batter. In 1869, Cornelius Swartwout patented the first stovetop waffle iron in the United States, making it easier to use on a range. The invention of the electric waffle iron in 1918 by General Electric further popularized waffles, turning them into a breakfast staple enjoyed by millions.

The Electric Fan: Beating the Heat

The electric fan, a device crucial for beating the heat, traces its origins to the late 19th century. In 1882, Dr. Schuyler Skaats Wheeler invented the first electric fan by attaching a two-blade propeller to an electric motor, providing a practical and efficient means of air circulation. This invention was a significant improvement over earlier mechanical fans, which were manually operated and less effective. Wheeler's electric fan quickly gained popularity, becoming a common household item and paving the way for the development of more advanced cooling systems, including modern air conditioning. The electric fan remains an essential appliance, valued for its simplicity and effectiveness in providing relief from hot weather.

The Stethoscope: A Doctor's Essential Tool

The stethoscope, an essential tool for doctors, was invented by French physician René Laennec in 1816. Initially, Laennec used a rolled-up sheet of paper to listen to a patient's heartbeat because he felt uncomfortable placing his ear directly on a woman's chest. This rudimentary device proved to be effective, prompting him to create a more permanent solution out of a wooden tube, which he called a "stethoscope" derived from the Greek words for chest and to view or examine. Laennec's invention revolutionized medical diagnostics, allowing doctors to hear internal sounds with clarity and leading to the development of the modern stethoscope, an indispensable instrument in healthcare.

The Disposable Diaper: A Parent's Convenience

The disposable diaper, a major convenience for parents, was invented by Marion Donovan in 1946. Frustrated with the inefficiency of cloth diapers and the rubber pants used to cover them, Donovan created a waterproof diaper cover using a shower curtain. She then developed a disposable absorbent pad, which evolved into the first disposable diaper. Initially, her innovation was met with skepticism, but it gained popularity after she patented it and later sold the rights to the Keko Corporation. Donovan's invention revolutionized infant care, providing a practical and hygienic solution for diapering that has since become a staple for parents worldwide.

The Ballpoint Pen: An Argentine Invention

The ballpoint pen, now an everyday writing instrument, was invented by Hungarian-Argentine journalist László Bíró in 1938. Frustrated with the smudging and inefficiency of fountain pens, Bíró, along with his brother György, an experienced chemist, developed a pen that used a tiny ball bearing in the tip to dispense quick-drying ink evenly and smoothly. This innovation provided a reliable and clean writing experience. The Bíró brothers' invention gained significant attention during World War II, leading to its widespread adoption by the British Royal Air Force because it could write at high altitudes without leaking. The ballpoint pen's practical design and functionality quickly made it a global success.

The Refrigerator: Cooling Down the Kitchen

The refrigerator, a kitchen essential, was not always a household staple. The first practical refrigerator was invented by Carl von Linde in 1876, using the process of liquefying gases to create cold temperatures. Before electric refrigerators, people relied on iceboxes, which used blocks of ice to keep food cool. The transition to electric refrigerators in the early 20th century revolutionized food storage, drastically reducing food spoilage and expanding the variety of available perishable goods. Interestingly, the early adoption of refrigerators also led to changes in kitchen design, as the convenience and efficiency of electric cooling transformed how people stored and prepared their food.

The Air Conditioner: A Cool Invention

The air conditioner, a revolutionary invention for climate control, was originally created to address a printing problem rather than for comfort. In 1902, Willis Carrier developed the first modern air conditioning system to help a New York printing company combat humidity issues that were causing paper to warp and ink to smear. Carrier's system controlled both temperature and humidity, significantly improving print quality. This invention's impact extended far beyond the printing industry, eventually transforming homes, workplaces, and entire cities by making indoor environments more comfortable. Carrier's innovation not only improved industrial processes but also led to the widespread adoption of air conditioning, fundamentally changing how people live and work in hot climates.

Play-Doh: Wallpaper Cleaner

Play-Doh, the popular children's modeling compound, was originally created as a wall-paper cleaner in the 1930s. The product was developed by Kutol Products, a soap manu-facturer, to remove coal dust from wallpaper. However, as homes transitioned from coal to cleaner energy sources, the demand for wallpaper cleaner declined. In the 1950s, Joe McVicker, a relative of the company's owner, discovered that the compound could be repurposed as a safe, malleable toy for children. Renamed and rebranded as Play-Doh, it was introduced to schools and then sold in toy stores, becoming an instant success and a beloved creative tool for generations of children.

The Traffic Light: Guiding Urban Traffic

The traffic light, essential for managing urban traffic, has an intriguing origin linked to railroads. The first electric traffic signal was installed in Cleveland, Ohio, in 1914, invented by James Hoge. However, an earlier, non-electric version was installed in London in 1868 and was operated manually with semaphore arms during the day and gas lamps at night. This design was inspired by railway signaling systems to prevent collisions. Although the London signal exploded a month after installation, the concept evolved. Hoge's electric version included red and green lights, eventually adding the yellow light for caution, creating the standard system that efficiently guides millions of drivers worldwide today.

The Vacuum Cleaner: Sucking Up Dirt

The vacuum cleaner, an indispensable household appliance for sucking up dirt, has its origins in a manually operated device called the "Whirlwind" invented in 1869 by Ives W. McGaffey. This early vacuum required the user to turn a crank while pushing the machine to generate suction. The first motorized vacuum cleaner was invented by Hubert Cecil Booth in 1901 and was so large that it had to be transported by horse-drawn carriage. Booth's design, known as the "Puffing Billy," involved long hoses being fed through windows to clean buildings. These innovations paved the way for the compact, powerful vacuum cleaners we use today, making cleaning more efficient and convenient.

The Sewing Machine: Stitching Together Innovation

The sewing machine, a revolutionary invention in textile manufacturing, had a tumultuous path to success. Although Elias Howe is credited with patenting the first functional sewing machine in 1846, it was Isaac Singer who improved the design and made it commercially viable. Singer's machine featured a foot pedal, allowing for continuous stitching without manual cranking. Interestingly, both inventors became embroiled in a fierce patent battle, which led to the establishment of the first patent pool in the

United States. This legal arrangement allowed multiple companies to manufacture sewing machines under standardized patents, significantly boosting production and accessibility, and ultimately transforming the garment industry.

The Elevator: Lifting Urban Life

The elevator, crucial for modern urban life, became safe and practical thanks to Elisha Otis's invention of the safety brake in 1852. Before Otis's breakthrough, elevators were considered too dangerous due to the frequent breaking of hoisting cables. At the 1854 New York World's Fair, Otis dramatically demonstrated his safety brake by cutting the elevator's rope and showing that the platform remained suspended. This innovation made elevators reliable and spurred the construction of skyscrapers, fundamentally transforming city landscapes by enabling buildings to reach new heights and making upper floors accessible and desirable.

The Bicycle: Pedaling Through History

The bicycle, a widely used mode of transportation and recreation, has undergone significant evolution since its inception. The first bicycle-like invention was the "Draisine" or "running machine," created by Baron Karl von Drais in 1817, which had no pedals and was propelled by the rider's feet pushing against the ground. It wasn't until the 1860s in France that pedals were added to the front wheel, giving rise to the "velocipede" or "boneshaker" due to its rough ride on cobblestone streets. The modern bicycle design, featuring a chain-driven rear wheel and equal-sized wheels, was developed in the 1880s and known as the "safety bicycle." This innovation made cycling more efficient and accessible, leading to its widespread popularity and impact on personal mobility.

Lysol: From Feminine Hygiene to Household Cleaner

Lysol, now well-known as a household disinfectant, originally served a very different purpose. In the early 20th century, Lysol was marketed as a feminine hygiene product, specifically as a contraceptive and a treatment for "feminine discomfort." Advertisements from that era promoted Lysol as a safe and effective method for preventing pregnancy, despite the serious health risks associated with such use. Over time, as medical understanding and regulations evolved, Lysol transitioned away from personal care and became widely recognized for its disinfectant properties, effectively cleaning and sanitizing surfaces in homes and hospitals worldwide.

The Computer Mouse: Navigating the Digital World

The computer mouse, a vital tool for navigating the digital world, was invented by Douglas Engelbart in 1964. Initially referred to as the "X-Y Position Indicator for a Display System," the first prototype was a wooden shell with two metal wheels, allowing users to move a cursor on a screen. Engelbart demonstrated this innovative device in 1968 during what is now known as "The Mother of All Demos," showcasing revolutionary computer technologies such as video conferencing and hypertext. The nickname "mouse" came about because the cord resembled a tail, and the term quickly caught on, leading to the widespread adoption of the mouse in personal computing.

Super Glue

Super Glue, a powerful adhesive, was accidentally discovered in 1942 by Dr. Harry Coover while he was developing clear plastic gun sights for the war effort. The substance he stumbled upon, cyanoacrylate, was initially dismissed because it stuck to everything it touched. It wasn't until 1951, while working at Eastman Kodak, that Coover and his colleague Fred Joyner realized the commercial potential of this exceptionally strong adhesive. Marketed as "Super Glue" in 1958, it gained fame for its ability to bond virtually any material almost instantly, revolutionizing household repairs and various industrial applications.

The Washing Machine: Cleaning Up Chores

The washing machine revolutionized household chores by dramatically reducing the time and effort required to clean clothes. Before its invention, laundry was an arduous task involving hand-washing garments in tubs or rivers, often taking an entire day. The advent of the washing machine not only mechanized this process but also introduced advanced features like spin cycles and different wash settings, making it possible to wash various fabrics more effectively and efficiently. This appliance significantly impacted daily life, offering convenience and freeing up time for other activities.

The Digital Camera: Capturing Moments

The first digital camera was invented in 1975 by Steven Sasson, an engineer at Eastman Kodak. This prototype weighed eight pounds and captured black-and-white images at a resolution of 0.01 megapixels. It took 23 seconds to record a single image onto a cassette tape, highlighting the early stages of digital imaging technology. Despite its rudimentary nature, this invention laid the foundation for the digital photography revolution, eventually leading to the development of compact digital cameras, smartphones with high-resolution cameras, and the widespread ability to capture and share moments instantaneously.

The Electric Guitar: Rocking the Music World

The electric guitar, introduced in the 1930s, revolutionized music by enabling louder and more versatile sound production. One of the earliest and most influential models was the Fender Telecaster, created in 1950, which set the standard for solid-body electric guitars. This innovation allowed musicians to experiment with new genres and styles, giving rise to rock and roll, blues, and countless other musical movements. Iconic guitarists like Jimi Hendrix and Eric Clapton utilized the electric guitar's capabilities to craft unique sounds that defined entire eras of music, cementing the instrument's place as a cornerstone of modern music.

Chapter Ten
Cultural Curiosities

Holi: India's Festival of Colors

Holi, India's Festival of Colors, is celebrated with vibrant enthusiasm and marks the arrival of spring. This ancient Hindu festival symbolizes the victory of good over evil and the end of winter. During Holi, people gather in open spaces to throw colored powders and water at each other, creating a joyous and chaotic spectacle of color. One of the key legends associated with Holi involves the triumph of the young Prahlad over the demoness Holika, which emphasizes the festival's theme of renewal and hope. Additionally, Holi fosters community bonds, as people from all backgrounds come together to celebrate, sing, dance, and enjoy festive foods.

Day of the Dead: Mexico's Celebration of Life and Death

Day of the Dead, or Día de los Muertos, is a vibrant Mexican celebration that honors deceased loved ones through a blend of indigenous traditions and Catholicism. Celebrated on November 1st and 2nd, this holiday transforms cemeteries and homes into colorful spaces adorned with marigold flowers, sugar skulls, and altars (ofrendas) filled with offerings such as food, drinks, and mementos of the deceased. One of the most recognizable symbols of this festival is the calavera, a whimsical skeleton figure often depicted in elaborate costumes. This celebration is not a time of mourning but rather a joyful occasion to remember and reconnect with the spirits of the departed, emphasizing the cyclical nature of life and death.

La Tomatina: Spain's Tomato-Throwing Festival

La Tomatina, held in the town of Buñol, Spain, is a unique festival where participants engage in a massive tomato fight. This event, which takes place on the last Wednesday of August, began in 1945 when a group of young people started a spontaneous tomato fight in the town square. Today, it attracts thousands of people from around the world who gather to throw overripe tomatoes at each other, turning the streets into a sea of red. The festival begins with participants trying to climb a greased pole to retrieve a ham, followed by an hour-long tomato battle. After the fight, fire trucks hose down the streets and participants, leaving the town remarkably clean due to the acidity of the tomatoes acting as a disinfectant.

The Maasai Jumping Dance: A Rite of Passage

The Maasai Jumping Dance, known as "Adumu," is a traditional rite of passage for young Maasai warriors in Kenya and Tanzania. This dance is a significant part of the "Eunoto" ceremony, marking the transition from boyhood to manhood. During the dance, young men form a circle and take turns leaping into the air, aiming to jump as high as possible without letting their heels touch the ground. The height of their jumps symbolizes strength and endurance, qualities highly valued in Maasai culture. Adumu is accompanied by rhythmic chanting and the deep, resonant singing of the warriors, creating a powerful and visually striking display of cultural heritage and communal identity.

Hanami: Japan's Cherry Blossom Viewing

Hanami, Japan's tradition of cherry blossom viewing, has been celebrated for centuries and signifies the arrival of spring. This custom involves gathering with family and friends under blooming cherry trees (sakura) to appreciate their fleeting beauty. The practice dates back to the Nara period (710-794), but it became widely popular during the Heian period (794-1185), initially among the elite and later embraced by all social classes. Hanami is not just about admiring flowers; it includes picnics with seasonal foods and drinks, poetry recitals, and sometimes even nighttime viewings known as "yozakura."

The ephemeral nature of the cherry blossoms, which typically last only a week or two, symbolizes the transient beauty of life, making Hanami a profound cultural experience.

The Highland Games: Scotland's Celebration of Strength and Culture

The Highland Games, a traditional Scottish event, celebrate strength, athleticism, and cultural heritage. Held annually in various towns across Scotland, these games include a variety of unique competitions such as caber tossing, where participants flip a large wooden log end over end, and stone put, similar to shot put but with a heavy stone. Dating back to the 11th century, the games were initially a way for clan chiefs to select their strongest warriors. Today, they feature not only athletic contests but also traditional music and dance, with bagpipe performances and Highland dancing adding to the festive atmosphere. The Highland Games serve as a vibrant showcase of Scottish culture, attracting visitors from around the world who come to witness these impressive feats of strength and endurance.

The Running of the Bulls: Pamplona's Thrilling Tradition

The Running of the Bulls, or "Encierro," is a thrilling and historic tradition that takes place annually during the San Fermín festival in Pamplona, Spain. Dating back to the 14th century, this event was initially part of the process of transporting bulls from the countryside to the bullring. Over time, it evolved into a daring spectacle where participants, dressed in white with red scarves, run alongside a group of charging bulls through the narrow streets of Pamplona. The run covers approximately 875 meters and lasts just a few minutes, but it requires significant bravery and quick reflexes. Each year, this adrenaline-pumping event attracts thousands of locals and tourists, who either participate in the run or watch from the safety of barricades and balconies.

Midsummer: Scandinavia's Festival of Light

Midsummer, celebrated in Scandinavia, marks the summer solstice with joyous festivities that honor light and nature. This ancient tradition, particularly vibrant in Sweden, includes raising and dancing around a maypole decorated with flowers and greenery, symbolizing fertility and the arrival of summer. Participants wear flower crowns, sing traditional songs, and enjoy feasts featuring herring, potatoes, and strawberries. Bonfires are lit to ward off evil spirits and to celebrate the longest day of the year. Midsummer's origins trace back to pre-Christian times, and its emphasis on light reflects the significance of the sun in cultures that experience long, dark winters. This festival not only celebrates the peak of summer but also fosters a strong sense of community and connection to nature.

Crying for Good Health: Japan's Naki Sumo Baby Contest

In Japan, the Naki Sumo Baby Crying Contest is a centuries-old tradition held annually at various temples, where sumo wrestlers compete to make babies cry first. This peculiar event is rooted in the belief that a baby's loud cries can drive away evil spirits and bring good health. During the contest, two sumo wrestlers each hold a baby and face off, employing gentle but exaggerated techniques to elicit tears, such as making faces or chanting. The baby who cries the loudest and first is deemed the winner, and the parents believe this will ensure their child's robust health and protection from malevolent forces.

The Royal Edinburgh Military Tattoo: A Spectacle of Music and Precision

The Royal Edinburgh Military Tattoo, held annually at Edinburgh Castle, is a spectacular event showcasing military bands, precision drills, and cultural performances from around the world. Established in 1950, this event has grown to become one of Scotland's most popular attractions, drawing thousands of spectators each August. One of the highlights is the massed pipes and drums, where numerous bagpipe bands perform together, creating a powerful and stirring musical experience. The Tattoo also features dramatic lighting and fireworks, adding to the grandeur of the performances. Each year, the show concludes with the haunting melody of a lone piper playing atop the castle battlements, a moment that leaves a lasting impression on all who attend.

Oktoberfest: Germany's World-Famous Beer Festival

Oktoberfest, held annually in Munich, Germany, is the world's largest beer festival, attracting millions of visitors from around the globe. This 16- to 18-day event dates back to 1810, when it began as a celebration of the marriage of Crown Prince Ludwig and Princess Therese. Today, Oktoberfest is renowned for its massive beer tents run by Munich's historic breweries, each offering their unique brews in liter-sized steins. The festival grounds, known as Theresienwiese, are filled with traditional Bavarian music, folk dances, and hearty cuisines like pretzels, sausages, and roast chicken. One lesser-known aspect of Oktoberfest is its opening ceremony, where the Mayor of Munich taps the first keg with a cry of "O'zapft is!" (It is tapped!) signaling the official start of the festivities.

Songkran: Thailand's Water Festival

Songkran, Thailand's Water Festival, marks the traditional Thai New Year with exuberant water fights and cultural rituals. Celebrated every April, this festival spans three days and involves people splashing water on each other as a symbol of purification and renewal. One unique aspect of Songkran is the use of scented water to gently pour over the hands of elders, seeking their blessings for the new year. In addition to the water activities, Songkran includes parades, traditional music, dance performances, and the cleaning of Buddha statues. Chiang Mai, one of the festival's most famous locations, transforms its streets into a lively battleground where locals and tourists alike join in the joyous celebrations.

The Siena Palio: Italy's Historic Horse Race

The Siena Palio, Italy's historic horse race, is a centuries-old tradition held twice a year in the Piazza del Campo. Dating back to the 13th century, this thrilling event features ten riders representing different city districts, or contrade, who compete bareback around the square's treacherous track. The race lasts only about 90 seconds, but its intensity and the fierce rivalry between contrade make it a spectacular spectacle. Each horse and jockey is blessed before the race, and the winning contrada earns not just a painted banner, or "palio," but also immense pride and bragging rights. The Palio's significance extends beyond the race itself, encompassing elaborate parades, colorful medieval costumes, and festive dinners, reflecting Siena's rich cultural heritage.

Mardi Gras: A Festive Prelude to Lent

Mardi Gras, celebrated as a festive prelude to Lent, is most famously associated with New Orleans, where it features vibrant parades, elaborate floats, and masked revelers. Rooted in ancient Roman and medieval European traditions, Mardi Gras was brought to North America by French settlers. One unique aspect of this celebration is the tradition of King Cake, a colorful pastry decorated with purple, green, and gold sugar, symbolizing justice, faith, and power. Hidden inside the cake is a small plastic baby, and the person who finds it must host the next party or provide the next cake. Mardi Gras also includes the wearing of intricate masks, which historically allowed people of all classes to mingle and celebrate without social constraints.

Lunar New Year: Asia's Most Celebrated Festival

Lunar New Year, Asia's most celebrated festival, is marked by a variety of traditions and festivities across countries like China, Vietnam, and Korea. One of the most recognizable customs is the use of red decorations, believed to ward off evil spirits and bring good fortune. The festival, which begins on the first day of the lunar calendar and lasts up to 15 days, features family reunions, feasts, and the exchange of red envelopes (hongbao) filled with money for good luck. In China, the Dragon and Lion dances are performed to scare away evil spirits and bring prosperity. Fireworks and firecrackers are also integral to the celebrations, creating a festive atmosphere and symbolizing the driving away of bad luck. The Lunar New Year culminates with the Lantern Festival, where communities come together to release lanterns into the sky, symbolizing the letting go of the past year and welcoming the new one.

The Viking Festival of Up Helly Aa: Shetland's Fiery Celebration

The Viking Festival of Up Helly Aa, celebrated in Shetland, Scotland, is a fiery spectacle that honors the islands' Norse heritage. Held on the last Tuesday of January, this festival features a torchlit procession of hundreds of participants dressed as Vikings, led by the "Jarl" and his squad. The procession culminates in the dramatic burning of a replica Viking longship, symbolizing the end of the yule season. Preparations for Up Helly Aa involve months of meticulous planning and craftsmanship, particularly in the construction of the longship and the creation of intricate costumes. This event not only showcases

Shetland's unique cultural identity but also fosters a strong sense of community spirit, as residents and visitors alike come together to celebrate and participate in the festivities.

Diwali: The Festival of Lights

Diwali, known as the Festival of Lights, is one of the most important Hindu celebrations, symbolizing the triumph of light over darkness and good over evil. Celebrated over five days, Diwali involves the lighting of oil lamps (diyas) and candles, decorating homes with colorful rangoli patterns, and setting off fireworks. One unique aspect of Diwali is the custom of exchanging sweets and gifts among family and friends, fostering a sense of community and joy. The festival also honors the goddess Lakshmi, the deity of wealth and prosperity, with prayers and rituals aimed at inviting her blessings. Diwali's origins are linked to several legends, including the return of Lord Rama to Ayodhya after a 14-year exile and his victory over the demon king Ravana, which is celebrated with immense enthusiasm and reverence.

The Mongolian Naadam Festival: A Celebration of the "Three Manly Games"

The Mongolian Naadam Festival, held every July, is a vibrant celebration of the "Three Manly Games": wrestling, horse racing, and archery. This ancient festival dates back to the era of Genghis Khan and showcases Mongolia's rich cultural heritage and warrior traditions. One unique aspect of Naadam is the participation of child jockeys, some as young as five years old, who race on semi-wild horses across vast distances, demonstrating remarkable skill and bravery. Wrestlers compete in traditional attire, performing an eagle dance before and after matches to honor their strength and agility. Archers, including women, demonstrate their precision with bows, often using traditional Mongolian recurved bows. The festival not only highlights these athletic feats but also includes elaborate ceremonies, traditional music, and colorful folk dances, creating a lively and culturally immersive experience.

The Balinese Day of Silence: Nyepi

Nyepi, the Balinese Day of Silence, is a unique and deeply spiritual celebration marking the Balinese New Year. Observed with 24 hours of complete silence, this day involves restrictions on travel, work, and even the use of electricity, as the entire island of Bali shuts down to meditate, reflect, and cleanse the past year's sins. One distinctive aspect of Nyepi is the ritual of the Ogoh-Ogoh parade held the day before, where large, intricate effigies representing malevolent spirits are paraded through the streets and then ceremonially burned to drive away evil forces. This transition from vibrant celebration to profound stillness symbolizes the renewal of life and the island's commitment to maintaining balance and harmony.

The Calgary Stampede: Canada's "Greatest Outdoor Show on Earth"

The Calgary Stampede, dubbed Canada's "Greatest Outdoor Show on Earth," is an annual rodeo, exhibition, and festival held every July in Calgary, Alberta. Originating in 1912, the Stampede has grown to become one of the largest and most famous rodeos in the world. A unique feature of this ten-day event is the free pancake breakfasts served throughout the city, a tradition that started in 1923 to create a sense of community and hospitality. The Stampede includes thrilling rodeo competitions, a grand parade, agricultural exhibits, concerts, and a vibrant midway with rides and games. The nightly Grandstand Show and fireworks display are highlights, drawing spectators from around the globe to celebrate Calgary's rich Western heritage and culture.

The Krampus Parade: Austria's Dark Christmas Tradition

The Krampus Parade, or Krampuslauf, is a dark and thrilling Christmas tradition celebrated in Austria and parts of Central Europe. Taking place in early December, this parade features participants dressed as Krampus, a fearsome half-goat, half-demon figure from Alpine folklore who punishes naughty children. One unique element of the Krampus Parade is the intricate and terrifying masks, often handcrafted by local artisans, which transform the wearers into menacing creatures as they march through the streets. Accompanied by loud bells and chains, the Krampuses chase onlookers and create a chaotic, yet exhilarating atmosphere. This event contrasts sharply with the typically jolly Christmas festivities, adding a touch of ancient folklore and thrilling excitement to the holiday season.

The Camel Wrestling Festival: A Unique Turkish Tradition

The Camel Wrestling Festival, held annually in the Aegean region of Turkey, is a unique tradition that dates back over 2,400 years. This event features male camels, specially bred and trained for wrestling, competing in matches to establish dominance. A distinctive aspect of the festival is the festive atmosphere, with local music, dancing, and feasts that accompany the wrestling matches. Each camel wears elaborate, colorful decorations, and the wrestlers are carefully matched based on their size and temperament to ensure a fair contest. The camels push and grapple with each other using their necks, and a match is won when one camel forces the other to the ground or out of the ring. This tradition not only highlights the skill and training of the camels but also serves as a significant cultural event, bringing communities together to celebrate their heritage.

The Wife Carrying World Championships: Finland's Quirky Contest

The Wife Carrying World Championships, held annually in Sonkajärvi, Finland, is a quirky and entertaining contest that draws participants from around the globe. Originating from a 19th-century legend, the competition involves male participants carrying their female teammates through an obstacle course featuring hurdles, sand, and water. The race's unique twist is the "Estonian carry," where the wife hangs upside-down on her husband's back, her legs over his neck. The winning couple receives the wife's weight in beer as a prize. This playful event, combining athleticism and humor, has grown into an internationally recognized sport, fostering camaraderie and fun among contestants and spectators alike.

The Albuquerque International Balloon Fiesta: A Sky Full of Colors

The Albuquerque International Balloon Fiesta, held every October in New Mexico, is the largest hot air balloon festival in the world, attracting hundreds of balloonists and thousands of spectators. One particularly captivating event is the "Mass Ascension," where hundreds of balloons take off in two waves, filling the sky with a stunning array of colors and shapes. The fiesta began in 1972 with just 13 balloons and has grown to feature over 500 balloons from around the globe. Another highlight is the "Special Shape Rodeo," showcasing balloons in imaginative forms like animals, castles, and popular characters, adding a whimsical touch to the festival. The Albuquerque International Balloon Fiesta not only celebrates the art and skill of ballooning but also transforms the skies into a mesmerizing display of creativity and color.

The Monkey Buffet Festival: Honoring Monkeys in Thailand

The Monkey Buffet Festival, held annually in Lopburi, Thailand, is a unique event dedicated to honoring the local monkey population. This tradition began in 1989 and is celebrated in November, attracting both locals and tourists. The festival involves preparing a lavish feast for the monkeys, including fruits, vegetables, candies, and even sodas, arranged in elaborate displays at the ancient Khmer temple of Phra Prang Sam Yot. The event recognizes the monkeys' significance to Lopburi, where they are believed to bring good luck and attract tourism. As the monkeys eagerly indulge in the buffet, the festival creates a lively and joyful atmosphere, celebrating the harmonious relationship between the residents and their primate neighbors.

The Cheese Rolling Festival: Gloucestershire's Daring Tradition

The Cheese Rolling Festival, held annually on Cooper's Hill in Gloucestershire, England, is a daring and eccentric tradition that dates back to the early 19th century. Participants chase a 9-pound round of Double Gloucester cheese down the steep and uneven hill, often tumbling and rolling in their pursuit. The first person to cross the finish line wins the cheese. The event, known for its chaotic and high-spirited nature, attracts competitors and spectators from around the world. Injuries are common due to the hill's challenging terrain, but this only adds to the festival's thrill and legendary status. Despite its risky nature, the Cheese Rolling Festival continues to be a beloved and adrenaline-pumping celebration of local heritage.

The Kukeri Festival: Bulgaria's Masked Dancers

The Kukeri Festival, celebrated in various parts of Bulgaria, features masked dancers performing elaborate rituals to chase away evil spirits and ensure a good harvest. Taking place between Christmas and Lent, this ancient tradition involves participants donning intricate costumes made of animal pelts, feathers, and bells, with large, often grotesque masks designed to frighten away malevolent forces. One of the festival's unique elements is the dancers' vigorous and rhythmic movements, which, combined with the cacophony of ringing bells, create an enchanting and somewhat eerie atmosphere. The Kukeri Festival not only showcases Bulgaria's rich folklore but also strengthens community bonds as villagers come together to partake in this vibrant and mystical celebration.

The Harbin Ice and Snow Festival: China's Winter Wonderland

The Harbin Ice and Snow Festival, held annually in Harbin, China, transforms the city into a dazzling winter wonderland. Known for its massive and intricate ice sculptures, the festival features full-scale buildings, monuments, and fantastical creatures carved from blocks of ice sourced from the nearby Songhua River. One of the festival's most striking aspects is the use of multicolored lights embedded within the ice, illuminating the sculptures and creating a magical, otherworldly glow at night. Visitors can explore life-sized ice castles, slide down ice slides, and even participate in ice swimming competitions. The Harbin Ice and Snow Festival, which began in 1963, has grown into one of the world's largest and most spectacular winter events, attracting millions of tourists who come to marvel at the extraordinary artistry and celebrate the beauty of winter.

The Burning Man Festival: A Desert Experiment in Community and Art

The Burning Man Festival, held annually in Nevada's Black Rock Desert, is a unique experiment in community, art, and radical self-expression. One of the festival's most iconic features is the construction and subsequent burning of a large wooden effigy, known as "The Man," which symbolizes the event's theme of ephemerality and renewal. Participants, referred to as "Burners," create a temporary city filled with art installations, themed camps, and interactive experiences, all guided by principles such as decommodification, participation, and leaving no trace. The festival, which began in 1986 on a San Francisco beach, has grown into a global phenomenon, drawing tens of thousands of attendees who immerse themselves in a week of creativity, self-reliance, and communal living in one of the most inhospitable environments on Earth.

The Gion Matsuri: Kyoto's Ancient Festival

The Gion Matsuri, held every July in Kyoto, is one of Japan's most famous and oldest festivals, dating back to 869 AD. Originally created to appease the gods during a plague, this month-long celebration features a series of events culminating in the grand Yamaboko Junko procession. The procession showcases elaborately decorated floats, known as yamaboko, which are beautifully adorned with tapestries, lanterns, and art pieces. One of the unique aspects of Gion Matsuri is the float construction; these towering structures are assembled without using nails, relying instead on traditional wooden joinery techniques. The festival also includes traditional music, street food, and the opportunity to see participants in vibrant kimonos, all contributing to a vivid display of Kyoto's rich cultural heritage and community spirit.

The Rio Carnival: A Spectacle of Samba and Celebration

The Rio Carnival, held annually in Rio de Janeiro, Brazil, is the world's largest carnival, known for its vibrant parades, extravagant costumes, and infectious samba rhythms. One unique feature of the Rio Carnival is the competition between the city's top samba schools, each performing elaborate themed shows in the Sambadrome, a purpose-built parade area. These schools spend months preparing, with thousands of dancers, musicians, and artisans collaborating to create stunning floats and costumes. The festivities also include street parties, or "blocos," where people of all ages dance and celebrate in the streets, creating an atmosphere of unity and joy. The Rio Carnival's blend of music, dance, and cultural expression makes it a dazzling spectacle that attracts millions of visitors from around the globe every year.

The Pushkar Camel Fair: A Vibrant Gathering in India

The Pushkar Camel Fair, held annually in the town of Pushkar, Rajasthan, is one of India's most vibrant and colorful festivals. This event, which lasts for about two weeks, originally started as a livestock trading fair but has evolved into a major cultural spectacle. One of the unique features of the fair is the camel beauty contest, where camels are adorned with elaborate decorations and jewelry, and judged on their appearance and grooming. In addition to camel trading and competitions, the fair includes traditional Rajasthani music and dance performances, artisan markets, and a variety of sporting events like camel races and tug-of-war. The Pushkar Camel Fair also coincides with the sacred Kartik Purnima festival, attracting thousands of pilgrims who come to bathe in the holy Pushkar Lake, making it a significant religious and cultural gathering.

The Batalla de Vino: Spain's Wine Battle

The Batalla de Vino, or Wine Battle, is a lively annual event held in the town of Haro, in Spain's La Rioja region. Celebrated on June 29th, the feast day of St. Peter, this unique festival involves participants dousing each other with red wine, turning the streets into a sea of purple. The festivities begin with a procession to the Hermitage of San Felices de Bilibio, where a mass is held. Afterward, the wine battle commences, with attendees using buckets, water guns, and any container they can find to splash wine on one another. The event concludes with a communal meal and dancing, embodying the joyful and communal spirit of Spanish culture. The Batalla de Vino not only celebrates the region's rich winemaking heritage but also offers a fun and immersive way for locals and visitors to come together in exuberant celebration.

The Konark Dance Festival: Celebrating Odissi Dance in India

The Konark Dance Festival, held annually in Odisha, India, is a vibrant celebration of classical Indian dance, particularly the Odissi style. Set against the stunning backdrop of the 13th-century Sun Temple in Konark, the festival takes place every December and attracts dancers and enthusiasts from across the globe. One unique aspect of the festival is its open-air amphitheater, which allows performances to take place under the night sky, creating a mystical ambiance. In addition to Odissi, the festival showcases other classical dance forms such as Bharatanatyam, Kathak, and Kuchipudi. The Konark Dance Festival not only highlights India's rich cultural heritage but also serves as a platform for preserving and promoting the intricate art of classical dance.

The Timkat Festival: Ethiopia's Epiphany Celebration

The Timkat Festival, Ethiopia's vibrant Epiphany celebration, commemorates the baptism of Jesus Christ in the Jordan River. Held annually on January 19th (or 20th in a leap year), the festival is marked by a series of joyful and reverent events. One unique aspect of

Timkat is the re-enactment of the baptism, where priests bless the waters of a pool or river, and attendees immerse themselves, symbolizing spiritual renewal. The festivities begin the night before with a procession carrying replicas of the Ark of the Covenant, known as Tabots, to a body of water. The following morning, after the blessing of the water, the Tabots are paraded back to their churches amidst singing, dancing, and feasting, creating a deeply communal and spiritually uplifting experience.

The International Sand Sculpture Festival: Portugal's Artistic Beaches

The International Sand Sculpture Festival, held annually in Pêra, Portugal, is the world's largest sand sculpture event, transforming the Algarve's beaches into a spectacular outdoor gallery. Known locally as FIESA, the festival features intricate and enormous sand sculptures crafted by artists from around the globe, using over 40,000 tons of sand. One unique aspect of the festival is its thematic focus, with each year dedicated to a different theme, such as mythology, famous landmarks, or popular culture, allowing artists to create imaginative and diverse works of art. These sculptures, some reaching up to 12 meters in height, are meticulously detailed and often illuminated at night, creating a magical and captivating experience for visitors. The festival not only showcases extraordinary artistic talent but also emphasizes the ephemeral beauty of sand art.

The Cherry Blossom Festival: Celebrating Spring in Washington, D.C.

The Cherry Blossom Festival in Washington, D.C., is a vibrant celebration marking the arrival of spring, featuring the blooming of over 3,000 cherry trees gifted by Japan in 1912. One unique aspect of the festival is the National Cherry Blossom Festival Parade, which includes elaborate floats, giant helium balloons, and performances by musicians and dancers, drawing thousands of spectators. The festival also highlights traditional Japanese culture through events like the Sakura Matsuri street festival, which showcases Japanese food, arts, and crafts. The picturesque cherry blossoms framing iconic landmarks such as the Washington Monument and the Tidal Basin create a breathtaking backdrop, attracting visitors from all over the world to witness the fleeting beauty of the blossoms and participate in the numerous cultural activities.

The Festival of the Sahara: Tunisia's Desert Culture

The Festival of the Sahara, held annually in Douz, Tunisia, is a vibrant celebration of desert culture and traditions. This festival, which began in 1910, attracts visitors from around the globe who come to experience the rich heritage of the Saharan people. One unique aspect of the festival is the thrilling camel racing events, where skilled riders showcase their speed and agility on the desert sands. The festival also features traditional music and dance performances, showcasing the unique sounds and movements of the region. Additionally, attendees can witness Bedouin wedding ceremonies, poetry recitals, and intricate displays of traditional crafts. The Festival of the Sahara not only highlights the resilience and creativity of desert communities but also offers an immersive cultural experience in the heart of the Tunisian Sahara.

The Goroka Show: Papua New Guinea's Tribal Gathering

The Goroka Show, held annually in Papua New Guinea, is a vibrant tribal gathering that showcases the diverse cultures and traditions of the country's indigenous groups. Established in the 1950s, the show takes place in the town of Goroka and attracts tribes from across the highlands and coastal regions. One unique aspect of the Goroka Show is the "sing-sing" performances, where tribespeople dress in elaborate traditional costumes adorned with feathers, shells, and face paint, and perform songs and dances that tell stories of their heritage. These performances create a mesmerizing display of cultural diversity and unity, with over 100 different tribes participating. The Goroka Show not only celebrates the rich cultural tapestry of Papua New Guinea but also fosters mutual respect and understanding among its many indigenous communities.

The Fête de la Musique: World Music Day

The Fête de la Musique, also known as World Music Day, is a global celebration of music that originated in France in 1982. Held annually on June 21st, the festival encourages musicians of all genres and skill levels to perform in public spaces, creating spontaneous concerts in streets, parks, and squares. One unique aspect of the Fête de la Musique is its principle of free performances, ensuring that all events are accessible to everyone and fostering a spirit of community and shared enjoyment. This musical event has spread to over 120 countries, making it an international phenomenon that turns cities into vibrant, open-air stages. The Fête de la Musique not only highlights the universal language of music but also promotes cultural exchange and unity through the joy of live performances.

The Lantern Festival: Lighting Up the Night in Taiwan

The Lantern Festival, celebrated on the 15th day of the Lunar New Year in Taiwan, is a mesmerizing event that lights up the night sky with thousands of glowing lanterns. One of the most enchanting aspects of the festival is the release of sky lanterns in Pingxi, where participants write their wishes and prayers on lanterns before releasing them into the sky, creating a breathtaking spectacle of floating lights. In addition to sky lanterns, the festival features elaborate lantern displays, traditional folk performances, and lion and dragon dances. The Lantern Festival marks the end of the Lunar New Year celebrations and symbolizes the shedding of the old year and the welcoming of new beginnings. The festival not only showcases Taiwan's rich cultural heritage but also fosters a sense of hope and renewal among participants and spectators alike.

The Edinburgh Festival Fringe: A Celebration of Arts and Creativity

The Edinburgh Festival Fringe, held every August in Scotland's capital, is the world's largest arts festival, celebrating a diverse array of performances including theater, comedy, dance, and music. Established in 1947, the Fringe operates on an open-access principle, allowing any performer with a venue to participate. This unique aspect has led to an eclectic mix of shows, ranging from experimental and avant-garde productions to mainstream hits. One particularly notable feature of the Fringe is its role as a launching pad for comedians and actors, with many now-famous performers getting their start there. The festival transforms Edinburgh into a vibrant, bustling hub of creativity, attracting artists and audiences from around the globe and making the entire city a stage.

The Kumbh Mela: India's Spiritual Pilgrimage

The Kumbh Mela, India's largest spiritual pilgrimage, is held every 12 years at four rotating locations: Allahabad (Prayagraj), Haridwar, Nashik, and Ujjain. This sacred festival draws millions of pilgrims who gather to bathe in the confluence of holy rivers, such as the Ganges, Yamuna, and the mythical Saraswati at Prayagraj. One remarkable aspect of the Kumbh Mela is its recognition by UNESCO as an Intangible Cultural Heritage of Humanity, highlighting its immense cultural and spiritual significance. The festival features a mesmerizing display of rituals, including mass yogic practices, religious discourses, and processions led by sadhus and saints. The 2013 Kumbh Mela in Allahabad set a record with over 30 million people participating on its main bathing day, showcasing the profound devotion and unity among the attendees.

The Pflasterspektakel: Austria's Street Art Festival

The Pflasterspektakel, held annually in Linz, Austria, is one of Europe's most renowned street art festivals, transforming the city into a vibrant open-air stage every July. This festival features an eclectic mix of performances, including acrobatics, mime, music, dance, and fire shows, performed by artists from around the world. One unique aspect of Pflasterspektakel is its emphasis on interaction and spontaneity, with many performances involving audience participation and impromptu street acts that blur the line between performer and spectator. The festival also includes workshops and a children's program, fostering creativity and engagement across all ages. Over three days, the historic streets of Linz come alive with color, sound, and movement, celebrating the diverse talents of street artists and creating a dynamic cultural experience for visitors and locals alike.

The Regata Storica: Venice's Historic Boat Race

The Regata Storica, held annually on the first Sunday of September in Venice, is a historic boat race that dates back to the 13th century. This event is renowned for its vibrant water parade and competitive races featuring various types of traditional Venetian boats, including the iconic gondolas. One unique aspect of the Regata Storica is the stunning pageant that precedes the races, with rowers dressed in period costumes re-enacting the welcome given to Caterina Cornaro, the Queen of Cyprus, in 1489. The main race, the "Campioni su Gondolini," sees skilled rowers navigating their slender gondolas along the Grand Canal, cheered on by crowds lining the banks. The Regata Storica not only showcases Venice's rich maritime heritage but also brings the city's history and traditions to life in a spectacular and engaging way.

The Basler Fasnacht: Switzerland's Carnival Celebration

The Basler Fasnacht, held annually in Basel, Switzerland, is the country's largest and most vibrant carnival celebration, known for its unique timing and traditions. Unlike most carnivals that take place before Lent, Basler Fasnacht begins precisely at 4:00 AM on the Monday following Ash Wednesday with the "Morgestraich," when the city's lights are extinguished, and colorful lanterns illuminate the streets. One unique aspect of Basler Fasnacht is its strict adherence to "Cliques," groups of masked participants who march through the city playing piccolos and drums, often performing satirical pieces that critique political and social issues. The festival lasts exactly 72 hours and features elaborate costumes, witty lantern displays, and confetti-filled parades. The Basler Fasnacht not only offers a rich display of Swiss culture but also provides a platform for artistic expression and social commentary, making it a distinctive and cherished event.

The Galway Oyster Festival: Ireland's Seafood Celebration

The Galway Oyster Festival, held annually in Galway, Ireland, is one of the world's oldest oyster festivals, celebrating the start of the oyster season each September. Established in 1954, this lively event is renowned for its oyster-opening competition, where participants from around the globe compete to shuck the most oysters in the shortest time. One unique highlight of the festival is the crowning of the "Oyster Pearl," a title awarded to the festival queen, who leads the opening parade. The festival features a variety of activities, including seafood tastings, cooking demonstrations, live music, and street performances, all set against the backdrop of Galway's picturesque coastal scenery. The Galway Oyster Festival not only showcases Ireland's rich culinary heritage but also draws seafood enthusiasts from all over the world to partake in its festive atmosphere.

The White Nights Festival: St. Petersburg's Cultural Extravaganza

The White Nights Festival, held annually in St. Petersburg, Russia, is a cultural extravaganza that takes advantage of the city's near-midnight sun during the summer months. Running from late May to early July, this festival features a plethora of events, including ballet, opera, music concerts, and theater performances. One of the festival's most iconic events is the "Scarlet Sails" celebration, a tradition that dates back to the end of World War II and marks the high school graduation season. During this event, a ship with red sails glides along the Neva River amid a spectacular fireworks display and water show, drawing massive crowds. The White Nights Festival not only highlights St. Petersburg's rich artistic heritage but also transforms the city into a vibrant hub of international culture and celebration.

The Mount Hagen Cultural Show: Showcasing Papua New Guinea's Diversity

The Mount Hagen Cultural Show, held annually in the highlands of Papua New Guinea, is a vibrant event that showcases the country's incredible cultural diversity. Established in 1961 as a means to promote peace among warring tribes, the show brings together over a hundred different tribal groups, each displaying their unique traditions, dances, and costumes. One particularly captivating aspect of the Mount Hagen Cultural Show is the "sing-sing" performances, where tribespeople adorn themselves in elaborate headdresses made of feathers, shells, and animal pelts, and paint their faces in striking patterns. These performances are not only a visual feast but also serve as a powerful expression of cultural identity and unity, drawing visitors from around the globe to witness the rich tapestry of Papua New Guinea's heritage.

The Aomori Nebuta Festival: Japan's Vibrant Parade of Floats

The Aomori Nebuta Festival, held annually in early August in Aomori, Japan, is renowned for its vibrant parade of enormous, illuminated floats known as "nebuta." These intricately designed floats, made of washi paper over a wireframe and lit from within, depict scenes from Japanese mythology, history, and kabuki theater. A unique aspect of the festival is the participation of "haneto" dancers, who dress in traditional attire and energetically dance around the floats to the accompaniment of taiko drums, flutes, and hand cymbals. The festival culminates with a spectacular display of fireworks over Aomori Bay, enhancing the magical atmosphere. The Aomori Nebuta Festival not only celebrates artistic craftsmanship and cultural heritage but also draws over three million visitors each year, making it one of Japan's most popular summer events.